Glimpses Into Reality

GLIMPSES INTO REALITY

▼

Josephine Joan Peyton

Writer's Showcase
San Jose New York Lincoln Shanghai

Glimpses Into Reality

All Rights Reserved © 2001 by Josephine Joan Williams

No part of this book may be reproduced or transmitted in any form or by any means, graphic, electronic, or mechanical, including photocopying, recording, taping, or by any information storage retrieval system, without the permission in writing from the publisher.

Writer's Showcase
an imprint of iUniverse.com, Inc.

For information address:
iUniverse.com, Inc.
5220 S 16th, Ste. 200
Lincoln, NE 68512
www.iuniverse.com

ISBN: 0-595-19945-3

Printed in the United States of America

To My Son Henry Alexander Williams III

Contents

Foreword ix
Chapter One—Creation 1
   Earth 3
   Fall of Man...6
   Before the Fall of Man 9
Chapter Two—Jesus 11
   The Earth is not Blessed 11
   What Do We Mean by Savior? 14
   Avatars 18
   The Essenes 24
   Jesus' School...28
   The Secret Teachings 35
Chapter Three—Religion 41
   Immortality...46
   Mysticism 48
   Prayer 58
   Angels 59
   Churchianity..62
   Beliefs of an Esotericist 63
Chapter Four—Evolvement..66
   Duality..74
      Sex 78
   Fate or Destiny 82

Chapter Five—Education 85
    Mission in Life *91*
    Meditation *92*
    Truth *96*
    Inspiration *101*
    The Classics *103*
    Thought Power *106*
Chapter Six—Teachers 108
Chapter Seven—Discipleship 120
    Service *128*
Chapter Eight—Organizations and Orders 136
    Group Work *136*
    Organizations *139*
Chapter Nine—Government 146
Chapter Ten—Weaknesses 152
    Pride *152*
    Greed *153*
    Self Interest *154*
    Crime *154*
    Inadequacy *155*
    Selfishness *155*
    Weak Resolve *156*
    Mock Humility *156*
    Cowardliness *157*
    Wrong Speech *157*
Chapter Eleven—Current Developments 159
    1940's-1960's *159*
    The Present *172*
    The Future *179*
Index 187

Foreword

Many years had my notebooks lain in my files. Through many relocations had I packed and unpacked them along with my other belongings. I took them with me from Providence to New York City to Redwood City, California.

When events in my life or in the world at large threatened to upset my equilibrium, I would pull the notebooks out and read them to stabilize my consciousness as an onlooker, from that near but distant, participating but impersonal, detached but compassionate point of view.

The notebooks were my personal, very private possession, and less than a half-dozen people have known of their existence and the fantastic circumstances under which they had been written.

It all started during the Second World War. As more countries were drawn into it and the more humanity suffered, the more my inner being cried to God to end the senseless waste of life, devastation of land, crops, and ruin of property.

Then I heard, and I do not remember from whom, that if one read all of the Psalms at one sitting, and without stopping, whatsoever one asked of God would be granted.

I came home from the cathedral one Sunday after attending Mass, took my Bible and read the Psalms from beginning to end. I wept as I read and held to the thought of divine intervention stopping the war immediately.

On I read through the afternoon and into the evening. As I drew to the end of the last Psalm, a wondrous calm enveloped me. There came a conviction that my prayer had been heard, and that I would be given answers that my soul sought.

I do not remember now how long a time elapsed between that Sunday and the morning I was awakened to hear marvelous things. Thereafter, morning after morning this peculiar kind of presentation continued after I had been brought out of deep sleep and lay drowsing, neither fully awake nor totally asleep.

After a few days, maybe a week and maybe less, as I tried to recall what I had heard, it occurred to me that perhaps I ought to write down some things I wanted to remember. And that was the start of my notebooks.

When I first sat up to take the notebook and pencil from the stand beside my bed, the voice receded and faded away as I focussed my consciousness totally on the physical. I had to learn to maintain that borderline state where I could hear well and write as fast as I could at the same time. It was not easy.

There seemed to be various distinctly different intelligences communicating with me. I sensed their difference by the ease or difficulty in my grasping the meaning of their communication.

There was one who told me the most and was the easiest to understand. In answer to my query regarding his identity, he said he was an abbot who had been connected with an abbey in England, and I think he said around 1500 A.D. His name sounded something like Merriot and there was something about Ayrshire. He also said that some manuscripts had been given to Notre Dame Cathedral in Paris, in 1527, which are still in the church archives, which contain truths of great importance.

Another communicator said he was a monk in a monastery in the Carpathians and that he was a Brother of the Holy Cross Order. I heard the name of St. Stephen but do not know whether it referred to the abbey or to the monastery.

There was one who spoke only of Jesus; and when his thought waves touched mine, identities were unimportant. I never even asked.

Briefly I sensed others now and then. But the three aforementioned had the most to say. Once I asked the English abbot if it would be possible for me to see him. And then I had a dream of a middle-aged, slender man of short stature who seemed between five and five and a half feet tall. He wore a white habit with the cowl thrown back. His very dark hair and eyes contrasted with the white of his raiment. He was holding a white book out to me. His face was so kind; his smile was so gentle; his eyes were so understanding…Yet, the face had much strength in its lean, almost aquiline structure.

It was very difficult, as I mentioned before, to maintain the necessary detachment from the physical to understand and to write physically at the same time. Another difficulty seemed to be a language problem. I will try to describe it. It was as if the communication was being given in a language that I do not understand in my waking physical consciousness. But, as I heard it in my half dreaming state, some part of me translated it into the form in which I wrote. Each of my communicators seemed to speak in a different language.

At times only one spoke to me. And at other times two, three, or more had something to say. My own rate of vibration and elevation of consciousness seemed the determining factor in the communicator contacted. Their distinctiveness was very apparent to me. For instance, to the monk, God was anthropomorphic. To the abbot, God was an Intelligence beyond even the grasp of the human mind. But the one who spoke of Jesus and the Christ raised my consciousness beyond the state of making distinctions.

However, I am positive that there was never any automatic writing on my part, and no use was made of my physical self by any outside agent. Sometimes I would drop off to sleep in the middle of writing a sentence. But never did my hand do any writing by itself. I was always aware of every word I wrote. If I dropped off to sleep, that was the end of the communication for the time being.

I knew nothing about many subjects of the communications at the time I wrote of them. Some subjects seemed too utterly impossible to believe, but I wrote anyway and marveled. I do not pretend to understand, or even to agree with what I do understand of all that has been told to me. I do not defend any of the statements.

The communications stopped suddenly before the war ended. They resumed for a while during the late forties and early fifties. After that, communication was infrequent.

Never had I thought that the writings in my notebooks would ever be made public. Yet, deep in my consciousness was the sure knowledge that I must make the writings available to all who ask for them.

The penciled pages were fading with the passage of years, so I set about copying everything. I was immediately faced with the problem of continuity. At times, a subject was only mentioned, while later it would be picked up time and again to be elaborated upon. During each communication period, various subjects would thus be considered. And since the copy I made was disjointed in this manner, I cut it apart and grouped the subjects together.

Thus, I fulfill my obligation to pass on any material that will contribute to humanity's evolvement of consciousness.

Chapter One

Creation

October-December 1939

There is one God from whom all creation emerged and in whom all creation ultimately will lose itself. It includes and embraces everything and is beyond the comprehension of the human mind. God is not a person. "He created man in His image," means that man has an inner essence which is Godlike. This essence of God is in all of His creation, but in man there is an intelligent comprehension of its presence in him.

March 30, 1963

In the beginning all was void, but the spirit moved upon the face of the waters. Know that this spirit is the creative force in the entire universe. It dwells in all that is. It dwells in animal and also vegetable and mineral and gaseous substances. This spirit is an intelligent force following laws that are eternal, everlasting and beyond the comprehension of man. While man is in his physical body he does not understand and indeed cannot comprehend this law of the ever present, which is eternity. That is something which is beyond his comprehension.

August 13, 1961

Consider the vastness of the universe. In God's mind it is but a small thing. Infinite though it may seem, between creations it is as nothing. Many years ago, it was thought that the universe was round and was expanding; in fact it is finite and is round. What lies beyond, no one knows. God is. Yes, the greatness of God's universe is incomprehensible to man's mind. But, should man send out his consciousness in space, it will come back after circumnavigating the whole of space. We are as if inside a sphere.

March 7, 1949

God has created universes before, and he will create them again. Which way can man turn to escape his fate? No place. He is bounded by the universe. It is a small place to God, but vast to man.

October 18, 1955

God proclaimed the universe a mighty plan of His illimitable consciousness. God's Plan for the universe is not a time and space affair exclusively. What lies beyond time and space is of more importance in the Plan than we can conceive.

March 26, 1963

God brought forth creation with one end in view. When creation manifested, waters were latent fire, as well. All is fire. We realize that the basis of creation is all one, only the expression changes. Come what may, there are no new things in the universe. In view of this truth, it is only the ramifications and combinations and recombination of cosmic elements that may present new manifestations. That is the wonder and the beauty of manifestations. Always ever new forms emerge.

June 26, 1960

God obeys laws of His own making, even as the least of His creations, and no one on Earth knows all the laws of His creation. Men have tried to fathom the meaning and purpose of creation, only to arrive at the conclusion that it is God's will to create the universe. It is much more than that, really, but one of the first things to realize is that the creation of the planets was not simultaneous with the creation of the universe. The planets, being part of the solar system, were created simultaneously with it, even as every solar system is created. And ages of solar systems vary.

June 30, 1960

"…The morning stars sang," says the bard, which is, incidentally, true. They do sing. Each heavenly body emits a sound as it travels through space, and each has a different keynote.

February 18, 1949

When tides roll, as they inexorably do despite men's affairs, they ring a note of grandeur that sustains the world. Many planets have notes of a chord, but the Earth has many more notes than other planets.

Earth
January 16, 1961

In the beginning, God made the world not separately, but with other works. Creation is still going on.

September 7, 1964

The Earth is an entity, a living being, an intelligence. The Earth's physical, three-dimensional manifestation is a very small part, vast as it is, to the whole.

February 19, 1948

When the Earth came into being, it spewed forth of its own creation some powerful images which are imprinted on its aura. That is what make the affairs of men so confused. That is the cause of the eternal struggle and fire.

January 18, 1966

Surveys of history shows eternal strife and battle in all facets of manifestation, be it mineral, plant, animal, or human. Love, kindness, and joy are attained in spite of the opposition that life on Earth manifests. For sheer savagery, nothing equals nature. When meekness manifests, it is soon destroyed. Each kingdom in nature is either prey or the predator.

April 5, 1955

Where there is preying and parasitism, superiority in some form preys on inferiority.

August 25, 1964

Let us consider the three kingdoms in manifestation on the physical level. Each kingdom feeds on the one below it, which sustains it. Each kingdom evolves also while it draws nourishment according to its own laws of manifestation and growth.

The mineral kingdom evolves from hylos (aggregate of undifferentiated matter) and grows by crystallization.

The vegetable kingdom feeds on and grows by drawing on the minerals contained in the soil or in water.

The animal kingdom feeds on and grows by drawing on the plants in the vegetable kingdom.

March 30, 1963

Each kingdom feeds itself upon the one below. Each kingdom has its own infinite variety and scheme of evolvement. The mineral kingdom grows and alters through crystallization and feeds the kingdom above it, which is the vegetable. The vegetable kingdom has its own infinite variety, from grass up to trees, and this feeds the animal kingdom.

April 5, 1955

Chemically, the world of matter is a combination and a recombination of various elements. There is only one element, and that element is broken down into one hundred and forty-four components. It is the combinations of the components which make up the material universe.

March 30, 1963

There is a duality in the scheme of things that comprises the three kingdoms. The duality is spiritual and material. In the mineral, the spiritual is gold and gemstones. In the vegetable it is scent. In the animal, transmutation is toward spiritualization and soul consciousness.

May 23, 1948

Gold and diamonds are the highest achievements of the mineral and stone kingdoms. The oak is the highest achievement of the plant kingdom. Man is the highest achievement of the animal kingdom. Inasmuch as man towers over them all and uses them all, he must make sure that his use of them is right. By right use is meant the right raising of vibrations of the article used. A degrading of articles used lessens their vibrations. Noble uses of them raises their vibrations. Abuse of animals makes them fierce and lessens their vibrations. Kindness to animals makes them gentle and loving and raises their vibrations.

May 23, 1948

Use of gold or silver as legal tender lessens their vibrations. Paper currency in place of metal is a boon to the mineral kingdom. The ultimate in use of metal is the subjection of it to fire—which purifies it by melting it and separating the impurities in the crucible—and then its being wrought into articles for use by man. When man wears gold objects upon his person, he permeates them with his warmth and vibration, thereby giving the metal the noble usage it deserves.

February 25, 1960

Gold is the color of the Sun, it is the color of thought, pure creative thought, and even the color of this metal holds a meaning. But it is its innate vibration which is important. The vibration of gold is so beneficial that it is one of the great mysteries of occultism. Gold's good influence is not written about. Gold holds a key to many things. It is important to have gold in the house, and the purest unalloyed state it is in, the better it is.

May 23, 1948

As far as animals are concerned, man's best service to that kingdom of nature is to teach an animal to follow orders in some sort of service. This develops an animal's reasoning powers, although these are very rudimentary, since the animal is a creature of instinct.

In the plant kingdom, of course, plants are used as food and are assimilated into the body of man. Wood is a plant which retains its characteristics while still being used by man in dwellings, furniture and utensils.

August 25, 1964

Now we come to the human kingdom, which feeds on the animal kingdom. On more detailed scrutiny we run into seeming contradictions and parasitic situations. We find plants feeding on other plants (mistletoe feeding on oak trees), animals preying on other animals, and humans feeding on animals. The reason for this was occasioned by the "Fall of Man."

When humanity achieves reintegration with God, the ferocity existing in nature will cease.

Fall of Man March 30, 1963

Originally man was created by God in an immaterial body—a spiritual body—and the Garden of Eden was a state of being, an Edenic existence.

Man has seven vortices of force, infinitely higher pulsations than can be measured with any instruments existing on Earth today. These vortices, their arrangement and interplay constitute a man in his spiritual body. The angelic kingdom has such bodies. When man was created by God, he had a positive and negative polarity. God separated the negative polarity (took Adam's rib out of his body) and created woman. But there came a warning from God not to partake of the Tree of Knowledge of good and evil—an electromagnetic force peculiar to this Earth and having also a positive and negative polarity, but very much lower in vibratory rate. Even as you can magnetize various materials by bringing them together, so did the same principle came into play at the so-called Temptation. The serpent force, which is this Earth's electromagnetic force, acts like a cohesive agent.

When Eve, the negative polarity creation of mankind, was magnetized by the serpent force, she could react to the Earth's force of what is good for man and what is evil when in material manifestation. Being of a negative polarity in the human kingdom, she could blend easily with the negative force of the Earth. Adam, or man, being of a positive polarity, could not respond to either the serpent force or the negative force of the Earth, by the nature of his vibrations. The only negative force he could respond to was Eve, woman, because her negative polarity was in harmony with his positive vibrations. Thus, he became magnetized through contact with her. This is told as a story in Genesis, understandable even to a child.

When the vibratory rates of Adam and Eve lowered, they could no longer contact God, only "hear" him. That is how humanity "fell" into a coat of skin, a human body, which had evolved from the animal kingdom until it stood upright.

Evolution has truth in it, too. But animal man did not begin having a human soul, as we know it today, until a body had evolved from the animal kingdom that could withstand the vibratory rate of the soul.

The human soul's task is now to evolve back to the Edenic state, and this is done through using the Christ force brought to the Earth and infused into its astral counterpart by Jesus.

February 22, 1949

A human being is nothing but a superior kind of animal until he awakens that within himself which will make him a real human and a man. A man is, of course, a being whose natural habitat is not within flesh. He was created to rule over nature and objective, three-dimensional creation; but he proved his inadequacy when he plunged into manifestation in the three-dimensional aspects of creation, became enamored of it and was tempted by the delights of it. But he did not realize that a condition of life in the three-dimensional world of being entails suffering, because that is not his natural habitat and a three-dimensional world is a restriction. When a creature or being exists in its natural habitat, there is nothing but sheer bliss and joy and an utter absence of any kind of sorrow or suffering. It is a terrific effort now for man to escape from this entanglement in objective manifestation and to rise out of it into the full free manifestation that is man's true expression. Of course, man will be greater for having gone through this experience.

January 26, 1960

When mankind fell into incarnation in physical bodies, this automatically set the wheels in motion for processes of its return back into the paradisiacal state of existence—but with something added, the added ingredient being knowledge. Knowledge is what the human souls wanted, and knowledge is what they got through lives of bitter experience. Physical life is very difficult.

February 20, 1960

God is conscious of everything, no matter how small. This is beyond the comprehension of man. It is almost like imagining the consciousness of a termite being aware of everything going on in the Empire State Building—and intimately aware, at that. There is a scheme or Plan in creation about where it is evolving, rather than to what it is evolving, and God only knows it. Man, in cultivating his expansion of consciousness, has caught glimpses of the laws and their exactness of operation in manifestation. This is a great improvement on how a man was when he first started manifesting in this three-dimensional world. In spite of what is said regarding man falling into incarnation on the physical plane of being, isn't it possible that God planned it that way and meant for man to fall into incarnation? Perhaps God needed man to forward the evolution of the lower kingdoms of nature. For instance, in the mineral kingdom man is getting ore out of the ground, refining it, and making things with it. This is an evolvement in that kingdom. What man cannot fashion, he transmutes it into a higher state. Man burns coal for heat, and also peat and petroleum. Everything he digs up or quarries he improves upon or uses somehow. This is what man is doing.

In the vegetable kingdom he is eating things, and making things out of inedible items. He uses wood for fashioning dwellings and for furniture, and for making utensils. He even uses such things as gourds, pine cones, flowers, etc., for decoration.

Also, man trains animals or uses them for food at certain stages of his and their evolvement.

September 18, 1959

When God ruled that mankind inhabit the Earth, a particular force rained on this small globe. This force is responsible for mind and the ability to know God or to experience Him.

August 5, 1961

When God made the worlds, humanity was an experiment. Will, given to man, is an experiment. All else works under law. Only man can go outside the law. Such is the state of things. In any event, the experiment is successful. Gradually mankind is learning to be adaptable to conditions as they are.

August 26, 1960

In many ways humanity is bringing to fruition what God had ordained from the beginning. A vast intelligence is proceeding according to plan and order, and humanity is an assisting factor.

Before the Fall of Man December 31, 1960

All is life in the universe. Every speck, every atom, every tiniest imaginable bit pulses with life of some sort, which always engenders activity. Action is the soul of life. In these days we cannot say that a stone is an inert mass—far from it, because even a stone pulses with life and activity. Think of this and know God, for God is life.

May 4, 1960

When the world was young and everything lay in a steaming jungle, there were only weird animals roaming the world. Meanwhile, humanity, as a race, was already on Earth, but in its four-dimensional stage.

May 22, 1960

Later, humanity evolved into gelatinous bodies, ovate in form. It did not matter what the atmosphere was. In each planet's atmosphere the same happens, and then sentient life solidifies and humanity manifests in the form best suited to the atmosphere and conditions of the planet. All life on all planets manifests in different forms. Things are not the same throughout the universe. Basically, things are the same, but the combinations and recombination of elements vary. Thus, life manifests throughout the universe.

July 24, 1960

There are two kinds of people on Earth. Those that evolved from the animal kingdom, and those that reached a particular level in some other planetary system and have come to this planet to carry on. There are quite a few who have come in from the outside. Those are recognized by their fineness of features and delicate bone structure. Incarnating on this Earth is not an easy path to take. The Earth is a hard school—one of the hardest in the universe.

May 4, 1960

Some had come from another planet to start taking bodies and to go on with their evolvement. Then, some of them had come from the moon when it was a planet, while some souls had even been animals who had completed their evolvement and had individualized enough to achieve human incarnation—a primitive kind of human, still a human. Incarnation had to wait until a body suitable enough could be fashioned, a body delicate enough to hold a human soul. This took almost a billion years.

Chapter Two

Jesus

The Earth is not Blessed   June 2, 1957

The subject of our Earth and its place in the cosmic scheme is of great interest for a variety of reasons. It is our physical "home." Our physical bodies are its product and are composed of elements constituting its physical, three-dimensional manifestation.

Mystics refer to our planet as not one of the "blessed" or sacred ones. What makes a planet blessed? What characteristic makes a planet blessed or nonblessed?

One learns that in the cosmic scheme any heavenly "family" composed of a Sun and its planets with their satellites, are also evolving. A nebula of gases gathers speed and congeals until solid, three-dimensional bodies assume shape. This is on the physical. Vibrations continue to slow-up; heat and light diminish until the planets no longer emit light, but reflect the light of the Sun. Thus, day and night manifest.

There are planets in our scheme which are so heavy and so solid that our Earth is like a gas in comparison. If some giant force could pack the atoms together in our planet until it became the size of a grapefruit, then our planet would be equal in structure to that of some heavenly bodies in space.

"As above, so below." Evolvement is a law of the cosmos. This evolvement comes from within a planet, plant, mineral, animal and human kingdoms. It is vibrational in nature. Sometimes, the frequencies of the vibrations are so fantastically high that there are no manmade instruments to measure them. The evolvement force seems to come from outside our solar system and is focussed in the Sun, which then emanates it. The Sun is a conductor of this force and we call it cosmic consciousness or Christ power, depending in which school we are being prepared for initiation or spiritualization by this force. This force is of the positive polarity.

Our planet is permeated by an electromagnetic force, which manifests in the negative polarity. Because the Earth, as an entity, is primarily of the negative polarity, it is called Mother Earth, or the feminine aspect of creation. The negative polarity and the positive are not balanced equally. Our Earth is primarily negative, and that is why it is not blessed.

Cosmic Wisdom created man on Earth in nonmaterial bodies to hasten the process of its becoming balanced. But humanity "fell" into physical manifestation and became tied to the negative force which manifests as sex power.

But, periodically, Cosmic Wisdom sends a Teacher to teach man how to free himself from this negative polarity, which is a destroyer. If the Earth fails in its evolvement it will be destroyed by the electromagnetic force. The Earth will become heavier and heavier and will rotate more and more slowly; and its orbit will gradually take it further and further out into space, unless it collides with another planet and is shattered, or both planets shatter.

In fact, the Earth already is slowing in its spin and is slowing in its orbit. It is drifting away from the Sun. If it is not shattered by collision with another planet, it will cast itself out into the "outer darkness," where the heat of the Sun will not reach it. Only the light will reach it and the Sun will look like the stars do to us. On the other hand, if the Earth balances the positive and negative forces within itself, it will be paradise, and the Earth will become "blessed." The even balance will be reached and it can then go on in its spiritualizing process.

Humanity was created and placed on Earth to aid the Earth by its positive polarity while humanity itself was manifesting in nonmaterial bodies. When humanity descended into material manifestation, it also became more negative than positive, and was caught.

February 22, 1949

The Creator, in His infinite understanding emanated a great force from Himself, a force which we call the Christ power, to redeem humanity. It is truly a Son which the Creator sent forth. When a human attains a certain inner growth and development, this Christ power enters and suffuses his being entirely. Yes, truly, man is then an even greater creation than he originally was. Will he pull up the created manifested world of three dimensions into a higher manifestation, too? Yes, for that is his mission. There is a constant striving to attain the center of being and become one with the Creator.

June 2, 1957

Redeeming "fallen" man became the prime concern of Wisdom, God, the Cosmic, or whatever one wishes to call Divine Law. The only way that man could be redeemed was through the Christ force. This had to be focussed through a human body, fine enough to act as a conductor. Such a human body was that of Jesus. He was the Way Shower and in His life demonstrated physically what man has to go through psychically to be "saved" from the negative electromagnetic force of the Earth. The electromagnetic force in himself is transmuted into a creative force, rather than its being a destructive force when left in its natural state.

When Jesus gave up the Christ force upon swooning on the cross, it permeated the astral body of the Earth. The Christ force interpenetrates the Earth to this day, and puts the negative power in restraint.

What Do We Mean by Savior? August 5, 1966

The electromagnetic force of the Earth is known esoterically as the serpent power and is the carrier of the negative polarity. The reason for its being called, the serpent power is that its vibratory nature is in harmony with the vibratory rates of the reptile kingdom of animal life on Earth. It is also in harmony with the sex force in humanity. And this is the basis of serpent cults, incidentally. Before Jesus, serpent power inhibited humanity's progress spiritually: it was detrimental, because man's purpose for being is spiritual progress and expansion of consciousness.

May 5, 1955

There are symbolical drawings of the Earth with a serpent encircling it. What does this mean? Our Earth, as a living entity, has an electromagnetic force and vibration which are inimical to all living things on it. This force is the creative energy possessed by mineral, plant and animal manifestations of life. Long, long ago, the mystics discovered that the animal having the most concentrated form of this energy is the serpent. The more concentrated the force, the more deadly the venom.

In a human being this force is the sex force. The fluid in which the germ or sperm for procreating is suspended carries the force. This fluid is so vital and so strong that it governs the miracle of creating another human body on the physical level—and the mental creativity of genius. And this is the basis of primitive phallic worship, where the consciousness is centered solely in the body and its sense pleasures.

However, when humanity lifts its consciousness to the solar plexus—then emotions reign supreme. But that is not its aim and goal. The aim is to lift that power still higher—and Jesus came on Earth to teach how to lift it at least as high as the heart. And love is the hallmark, or should be, of Christianity. Love, forgiveness, and understanding result when the power of the creative energy is lifted to the heart. But that is not the end of the matter, either. The energy of that creative sex force has to be lifted even higher, to the head centers. The ancient Egyptians symbolized this miracle occurring in a human being by their headdress. The headdress shows that the serpent power has been transmuted into mental creative energy, and the fangs are drawn—they have no more power to harm or kill.

The esoteric symbol of a serpent uplifted has its fangs drawn out—not showing—and the eye of the serpent is blue—not black. The serpent is blue—not green and brown—but blue.

That is the positive aspect of the serpent.

There are still individuals with subconscious race memories of dim and distant incarnations in the past when they were part and parcel of the negative aspect of this serpent power and its terrible force. Negatively, this force manifests in greed, envy, maliciousness. It is a power used as a carrier of destructiveness.

Individuals who have discovered how simple and easy it is to generate this power within, and to use it for self-betterment, are sowing the seeds of their own destruction. They become helpless, and, eventually—once they open the lid within themselves for this electromagnetic force which the Earth is constantly generating—they absorb it into their systems; and in trying to get rid of it, they throw it off on anyone they can. They use energy to do this—energy of the serpent power as radiated by the Earth.

Energy depends on radiation rather than motion. Radiation transfers energy. Alterations in this energy pack atoms together.

June 2, 1957

From time immemorial, mystics have known of the electromagnetic power of the Earth, which manifests on Earth in all that lives. It is the sex force.

The percentage of individuals who have transmuted the energy of this force to the head centers is very, very small.

For thousands of years, the electromagnetic power, concentrated in the serpent had been used, negatively, since it was discovered that it could be used psychically as a carrier. The lone voice of Amenhotep IV tried to call humanity out of its toils into the realm of light. He lost, and for thousands of years humanity struggled.

God in His Wisdom sent One who could focus the Christ power in His Person to do battle with the insidious negative serpent power. Without hesitation, it can be said that the major uses of the serpent power is negative. However, there is protection one can use against it. This protection is the Christ power.

April 19, 1960

When humanity prays that Christ manifest, its prayers must perforce be answered. Consider the needless suffering of millions because they do not know of Christ protection. This power of God is ready and waiting in reserve and can be used by any and all.

August 5, 1966

We associate the term "Christ" with Jesus. We are also told that Jesus was the last and greatest Avatar. We are told that the Christ force, or power, descended into Him during his baptism by John. The Christ was seen as a dove over Jesus' head at the time of His baptism. Thereafter, He became Jesus, the Christ.

Starting with this premise, we can consider it piecemeal. Christ, as a power or a force, implies a vibratory agent. We are now familiar with the structure of an atom. It has a nucleus and electrons spinning around the nucleus. Therefore, the "dove" would be the picture of how this particular force manifests with its elongated lines of vibration, roughly in the shape of a cross, with the longest extension upward. It has two curves of infinity intersecting and interchanging—one vertical, and one horizontal.

This power is extraterrestrial. In fact, it comes from outside our solar system. The origin of it is in the region of Andromeda. It can only be drawn into a vehicle, a body, duly prepared to receive it, and this was provided by Jesus. His being irradiated by the Christ force gave Jesus the great power to manifest as a Healer, Teacher, and Savior.

August 5, 1966

When Jesus swooned on the cross at His crucifixion, he breathed out the Christ force, which then permeated the electromagnetic force of the Earth and inhibited its serpent activity.

From that day, the Earth is continually drawing the Christ force to itself, and it is available to all. And that is why Jesus is known as a Savior—because of this great service to mankind.

It is of interest to note that the signature of Christ is the Greek X (Chi) and P (Rho). Intoning Chi (pronounced Khai) and Rho on one's own individual keynote has stupendous effects.

In the Roman Catholic symbolism there is an interesting illustration concerning serpent force subjugated. It shows the Virgin Mary standing upon the world around which there is a serpent entwined, and She has Her foot upon the serpent's head.

Pursuing this analogy, we can see a series of meanings. Mary symbolizes mind in man. It is the mind of man which conceives the Christ in the heart (a Virgin Birth), where the Christ grows, and is fed on the milk of human kindness, as it were. The mind of man, when it achieves Christhood, subjugates the negative electromagnetic force of the Earth and keeps it underfoot.

The Christ force enters a human through the top of the head (the mind, Mary) and irradiates the whole being, with the heart as the focal point. That is the reason Jesus is sometimes pictured with a heart emitting rays. In Catholic symbology this is the Sacred Heart of Jesus.

Since man's physical self is of the Earth—earthy—the serpent power of it is in tune with him through his sex nature. The problem to humanity is that the serpent force is a destroyer—a devourer—until the Christed individual gains control over it.

October 29, 1955

Christ is a spiritual power which permeates, or rather, can permeate a physical body which has been prepared to accommodate it. Where there are two distinct powers, they cannot occupy the same body at the same time. One must go to make place for the other.

In the average human body the other power is that of the "beast." Definitely, the Christ is in every man, when he is ready, whether he is a Christian, Muhammadan or Jew. Progress of soul evolution cannot take place otherwise.

October 7, 1955

The glory of mankind depends upon the inner development and evolvement out of the animal stage into the truly human, which can be done only by the Christ power. The Christ power, the Son of God, is the mediating force between God and man. And when it says, "God so loved the world, that He sent His only begotten Son," it refers to the Christ power.

This power can only manifest when the individual has made his deliberate choice and decision to dedicate his life to God. Thus, and only thus, can man progress to reintegration with God. Only through Christ can this come about.

The Christ power manifests in pure form in an individual once every two thousand years. Therefore, it does not matter really who the person is or what faith he professes; it is still the Christ who saves him. That is why peoples of all faiths have a mediator to whom they address their prayers. Now the Jews will point out that they address their prayers to God and not to any mediator. And here is something which will startle not a few: all the peoples of the Earth are working for reintegration with God except the Jews. They are without the Christ principle because of choice. They choose the Earth and the manifestations upon it in all its fullness of good as their highest aim and achievement.

Avatars April 26, 1960

Long aeons of time had passed over the Earth's surface and all upon it before it was ready to harbor creatures like mankind. Then long ages passed before mankind was ready to grasp the realization of his own potential, although periodically "Sons of God" had been born on Earth to give mankind some sort of a religion and philosophy so that mankind could live a more useful life and accomplish greater strides forward. More is accomplished when mankind works in groups than singly. Man is a gregarious creature by nature. He is a social being to begin with, and must work with his fellow man to achieve the greatest effect.

October 21, 1955

Once in about two thousand years, particular forces pour into the space occupied by our solar universe and set up a chain reaction, the result of which produces in humanity the birth of one individual who revolutionizes the philosophy of life in mankind for the following two thousand years. Such a birth was that of Jesus, called the Christ. The forces of Saturn and Jupiter in conjunction in Pisces brought the heavy, irresistible force of the combined vibrations to play upon our small Earth. They made it possible for a soul of an extremely high vibratory rate to penetrate the dense materiality of our world and to take on physical incarnation. Other forces had been in operation previously, paving the way as it were, and preparing the climaxing event of the birth of an Avatar to occur.

Creation demands a redeeming power allowing for further growth and expansion, which manifests itself in the human kingdom periodically in the birth of an Avatar. Each such birth has brought a set of rules into operation which were prescribed as a guide to humanity. By following these rules humanity advances in its inevitable progress toward spirituality. The rules set forth are the right ones for the particular stage of evolvement toward spirituality that humanity as a whole has reached. Should the people not all be readied for a new Avatar's particular teaching, a modification of rules, and perhaps a new set of rules is devised and given forth through a subsidiary source. However, the lesser rules will have the same vibratory force as the original, but may be an octave or so lower. The condition and responsive mechanism of a particular people will make that necessary.

October 25, 1955

God brings many blessings to light that humanity sometimes undeservedly has. Therefore, the particular orientation of the Earth in the heavens makes the streaming in of cosmic rays of a particular kind possible and setting up of vibrations whereby an Avatar can appear.

Go forth and preach the everlasting unity, says Divine Wisdom to each Son of God as He comes on Earth every two thousand years and manifests the Christ power along the lines of the new age which he heralds.

Each new age has its own particular characteristic and different approach to life. A different philosophy evolves. A different set of values prompts humanity into a different pattern of evolvement. The Piscean age was that of Jesus, and all His teachings allowed for the particular forces raining in upon the Earth during the Piscean age.

In following Jesus' teachings, most benefits were derived in attaining cosmic consciousness and redemption from the necessity of rebirth. What Jesus taught had particular value to that portion of humanity which had assimilated all the teachings of the previous Avatar of the previous age and were ready for the next one. During the age that followed, the Jews, Buddhists and Muhammadans were not ready for it.

Although Muhammadanism came later, it is really only a new presentation and statement of the Hebrew religion. Hebraic law was for that segment of the Semitic race. The people who embraced Muhammadanism are of Semitic origin. And they were not quite ready to receive the higher vibratory applications of laws as Jesus set them forth. Hebraism is involutionary into materialism. Christianity is evolutionary into spirituality. Firm adherence to Hebraic tradition and law will inaugurate a new set of vibrations in a new octave, which opens the door for the influx of Christ power, and the Jew becomes a Christian. His next incarnation is into Christianity, in which faith he can make great strides by having learned the law of application. Humanity is very much retarded and many souls in Christianity are not ready for the teaching of the new Avatar who will manifest.

Thus far, Christianity is the highest pathway to reintegration with God.

October 20, 1955

God so loved the world that He sent His only Son to aid humanity. These words embody a world of truth undreamed of by theologians and students of the Bible. When humanity needs an Avatar it will invent one, as indeed it has in ages past. A web of legend has been spun around some figure, and humanity has worshiped it. The personalities involved may have been law givers inspired by God to set up certain laws for better living. Again, these personalities may have set forth explanations of phenomena puzzling mankind. They may even have been superb healers. All these things have set apart such personages from the common run of humanity. At first they were admired and respected, and after a time had hallowed their memory, they were deified. But they were not Avatars.

May 22, 1960

Gods of the ancients are really perfected Beings of a particular genus.

October 20, 1955

An Avatar is a highly esoteric truth. It actually is a cosmic law established when humanity had gotten a coat of skin (physical body on Earth rather than an etheric body in the paradisiacal state of existence). Such an One is conceived immaculately and is born of a virgin. Then, at a particular age, the Christ power infuses him after he has undergone a period of intense training. The mistake that modern man makes is to aver that Jesus was the only Avatar. This is not so. There have been Avatars who preceded Jesus, but Jesus was the latest and greatest of them all. The Son of God appellation refers to the Christ power which is the one and only and there has been no other. This Christ power infuses an Avatar, who reflects it perfectly. The greater the perfection of the reflection, the greater the Avatar. And the world had never known a greater reflection of the Christ power by any individual than that of Jesus.

This power descended on Jesus at the time of his baptism and departed when he fainted on the cross. Contrary to established tradition, Jesus did not die on the cross. Some day the truth of that will be known. What He did was to give up the Christ power with which He had been infused. This Christ power infused the etheric body of the Earth and is as much alive on Earth today as it was then in Jesus. And this Christ power is available to men to become even as Jesus was, and to do things equally to if not greater than Jesus did. This is the law of the Christ power.

And this power manifests in Avatars or beings born for the purpose of bringing ever higher laws and principles of manifestation to humanity's attention.

Man is a unique creation of God and the Christ power is the force which will eventually make men the true Sons of God.

April 18, 1948

Greatness of mind includes greatness of soul. Usually a highly vibrating soul will use a superior mind. Many such souls on Earth today owe their standing to wisdom in choosing and fashioning vehicles in which to manifest.

Slow advancement is ideal with most of the human race, but means are given for a rapid recapitulation of knowledge to a soul which has taken on a body for a purpose. When a soul wishes to incarnate on the Earth plane and no suitable vehicle can be found, The Holy Ghost, as It is sometimes called, is sent down to fashion a body for a high soul. It is all a great process involving atomic energy and spiritual power, invoked by a geometric symbol and playing of rays of vibrations on the female thus honored to bring forth a vehicle for the Savior, as this type of soul is sometimes called. This happens only once every two thousand years.

June 20, 1960

People have merited consideration through their prayers and entreaties for God to listen and again send an Avatar on the scene to enlighten and reveal to humanity a little more of the higher truths—truths which may not have been understood except by an exceptional few—when Jesus preached. Understand this: When Christ manifests, He always manifests in a different way. Jesus is now of the elite on the right hand of God and will not come back to Earth. But, the Christ, which is a power, will manifest through a Chosen One and give mankind a pattern of life for the next, the Aquarian age.

March 20, 1949

Souls need a gradual change in vibration to raise them an octave higher each time.

When He comes, humanity will not know Him. Only a scattered few will learn about Him and come to see Him out of curiosity. Otherwise, there will not be a sudden change in the tempo of living in the world.

Change will be gradual but effective. Many souls are ahead of the times and living the life which will be a normal state of affairs in time to come.

We can know only so much, but revelations come revealing the full import of how will and faith can work toward a realization of ideals.

December 13, 1967

When the new Avatar comes, all will not be ready for His very highly advanced teachings. Even as there are today religions predating Christianity, whose devotees are using their methods for inner growth and evolvement, so will current Christianity and Judaism, with its offspring, Muhammadanism, continue. However, Jesus wills that Christians unite under one banner of Rome, even as they are all united on the inner planes of being.

As more individuals awaken inwardly, they will forge ahead to Splendor on the Middle Path.

October 27, 1955

All religions perform this service to humanity. They teach a code for living, a code of morals, laws for behavior, and a method of approach to God. By this the soul evolves to cosmic consciousness out of, or rather beyond, being self-conscious. It is a great step forward, as great as that taken from being only a conscious creature to being a self-conscious one.

Perhaps, the greatest uniqueness in Jesus' teachings is that the individual must do all the work alone. No one helps him in a literal crucifixion of spirit upon the cross of matter. In fact all the episodes in the recorded life of Jesus are examples of what each and every individual goes through in the spirit to attain spirituality.

Nothing can stop the forward flow of evolution. There may be obstacles set up by evil forces to retard it, but nothing can actually stop it. From this we can see and judge exactly how much a person, or even a nation or a race has progressed to cosmic consciousness.

From the Annunciation to the Transfiguration, the process described is that of every soul on Earth on its way to attainment of God consciousness. And the beauty of it is that a soul can shorten the process of its evolvement out of matter into spirituality by countless lives. Specially is this important at this time, since humanity is very far behind schedule, as it were, in its achievement of cosmic consciousness and reintegration with God.

Buddhism should have achieved its mission long before this, but it is still making an uphill struggle against opposing forces. Christianity has almost run its allotted course. Its effect as a whole is not even up to the Baptism stage, exemplified by the Baptism of Jesus in the river Jordan and the descent of the Holy Spirit into Him.

The Essenes October 22, 1955

There was in Palestine a small group of people who called themselves the Essenes. The Greek speaking people of those days called them the Therapeuti. They were mostly known to the world by their dress and by their healing activities. They dressed in white, lived in separate communities by themselves and did not mingle socially with the outside world. But they helped where help was needed. Their healing was a combination of physical and metaphysical methods, depending on the evolvement of the patient and the nature of the malady. These Essenes were a strict semi-monastic order for both men and women and they lived a communal life, sharing everything. No one actually owned anything.

October 23, 1955

Thus, we know the family background of Jesus. He came from the Essenes. His mother and father's people were members of that sect, which outwardly professed the Jewish faith but practiced occultism by having learned the secret, esoteric truths underlying the Hebrew religion. Mary was the daughter of a priest and had been dedicated to God since childhood in service to the temple as a vestal. In reality, it took three generations to prepare a physical vehicle of sufficient purity for the Christ to manifest on Earth. The purifying process started with Mary's grandparents, both sets. And when Mary was twenty-one, having finished her service as vestal at the Essene temple, a High Master appeared to her. He informed her that she had been made pregnant immaculately and had been selected as a mother to have a Virgin Birth of an Avatar.

Mary had been told that a husband would be provided her, and she was also told what the name of her child was to be.

Meanwhile, all esoteric and monastic orders had been alerted that an Avatar was coming. In fact, an Essene named John had been sent into the world to preach the coming of an Avatar and to prepare the people. He was given, by the Masters, the power to baptize by water. That ritual was the signature of the new Avatar, who was coming to herald in the Piscean age to humanity. And the age lasts a little over two thousand years. All humanity had been prepared psychically. The impression had been made on people on the astral plane. Great was the rejoicing, therefore, at Jesus being born.

The world at large had been informed by astrologers and by other esoteric organizations of the Essenes that some such event was pending. Even the court astrologers of the king informed him of the unusual and significant conjunction that would take place, and they explained to the king what it meant.

Being very jealous of his power, the king consulted with the astrologers as to the best method to secure his throne. And the slaughter of the innocents was the result of such conferences.

But the Masters had foreseen just such an event and were prepared. In fact, the souls in incarnation as babes which were slaughtered received new bodies almost immediately and became the multitude which followed Jesus during His ministry.

October 31, 1955

Only the Essenes knew that one in their midst had been selected to bear an Avatar. They also knew it would be a Virgin Birth and they cast about for a suitable man to espouse the maid when her days commenced in which she conceived psychically.

Various men offered themselves at the temple and were told that one of the invisible Masters of the White Brotherhood would appear to the one who was selected. And so it happened. Joseph, the town carpenter, who was a true and humble Essene all his forty-odd years of life, was selected.

A High One of the Brotherhood appeared to him to inform him that his would be the honor and that he would name the new Avatar "Yeshua." And so it was.

As Mary's days grew near, the local government sent forth word that there would be a census taken for tax purposes. Every head of a household should go to the place of his birth.

There was no choice but for Joseph and Mary to make the trip, which they did. The Essenes along the way to Bethlehem, where Joseph had to go, were informed of their passing through and were enjoined to be hosts. The trip was made by donkey in very easy stages and all was well till they neared Bethlehem, where there were no Essenes at the time.

November 1, 1955

But that was as it should be, too, since Jesus was supposed to be born in a stable. The whole of Jesus' life was supposed to be a symbol, a pattern, or an exact example of what every human being has to go through in spirit to attain to the kingdom of heaven within, or reintegration with God.

October 8, 1955

When Jesus was born the whole colony of Essenes took a hand in His upbringing. Mary, Jesus' mother, started normal married life with her husband and in time Jesus had two brothers and three sisters. Jesus was under the tutelage of the priests in the Essenian community, and it is small wonder that he astounded the Rabbis in the outer Jewish temples. The Essenes followed the Jewish religion outwardly. Judah and Israel were two different peoples. The Israelites were the Essenes, of whom Jesus was born.

May 9, 1960

When Jesus was twelve years old and ready to prepare for the ceremonies at the temple, he knew that long years were to be spent in learning how to control the vital life force and in knowing how to heal. That is how the miracles were done. It is necessary to know which force blesses and heals and which force destroys what. Perfect control is necessary.

October 24, 1955

Under many circumstances, the broad applications of occult laws are not known and many aspects of Jesus' life are puzzling until one learns these laws and realizes that it could not be otherwise. There is nothing truly miraculous about Jesus' life. All is directly simple and wholly natural, and also inevitable, when one understands the occult significance of everything.

April 24, 1960

Long preparation was necessary by Jesus to be able to launch this new approach to a method for the real man to benefit from his experience of living in the flesh. Great effort was expended by the Hierarchy of Great Souls to help Him in formulating a plan of action which would have the greatest telling effect on humanity. This brought a great amount of activity, not only in Jesus' life but on the higher planes and dimensions of existence.

November 5, 1954

God sent the Christ manifestation to humanity to teach humanity that there is a way to attain conscious immortality and a permanent vehicle of manifestation. Humanity is to take each recording of Jesus' life and use that as an example of everything that each individual must experience to attain illumination. When the record states that Mary gave birth in a stable, one must realize that it is an illustration of the fact that the Christ consciousness is born in animal man, among animals, which most of humanity is, in effect.

The next episode relates to the visit of the Three Kings bearing gifts. This means that every time the Christ consciousness is born within an individual he receives three gifts from God. These are real gifts which the individual puts to use.

Properly speaking, the birth of Jesus presaged a new era, the era of the Christ dispensation. It accelerated the process of man's evolvement from mere self consciousness to God consciousness or cosmic consciousness. There is as great, if not a greater step between a conscious being and a self-conscious man as there is between a self-conscious man and a God-conscious human. Man is still an animal until he becomes a human. And the only way he can become a human is to attain Christhood. A large order. That is why there are so few humans in the world.

October 28, 1955

When Christ brought illumination into the world through embodiment in the man Jesus, it was a great step forward for humanity. Working along mental lines, it produces blood transfiguration by irradiating each corpuscle. Seldom does an experience of complete transfiguration occur on Earth; and when it does, it is epochal. God makes it possible for man to attain immortality consciously, that is, a continuous immortality linking the physical consciousness with the spiritual.

November 1, 1955

Up to the time of Jesus, Initiation took another form. The Initiate underwent various experiences bodily, but Jesus redeemed humanity from that necessity and took it all upon himself. If for nothing else but just for that alone, humans should be the most grateful beings in the universe. Not just for one individual, nor for a nation, nor for a race, but, think of it, for the whole of mankind! By Jesus going through the experiences that He did, you and I do not need to suffer physically to attain reintegration with God. Our experiences will be only in spirit and our immortal souls will reenact Jesus's life in every particular, but the body will be spared.

Jesus' School October 22, 1955+April 26, 1960

When Jesus came on Earth there was an overwhelming amount of sin. The accumulation of sin was so great that evil forces operated openly. Corruption in everything was the order of the day. People were incredibly selfish, unfeeling, cruel and really criminal, and totally material. People were only interested in their own well-being and followed only those who would benefit them in some way. From the highest official to the lowliest stable worker, honesty, integrity, and consideration for the rights of others were foreign, unpracticed virtues. Everyone acted the way he did for self-protection. If one was not quick and clever and an opportunist, one was lost. It was small wonder that the teachings of Jesus seemed to be madness of the first order.

And that was the general condition in the world which prevailed also in Palestine under Roman rule.

April 23 & 26, 1960

Jesus had a tremendous task before him. The people were oppressed, had very few joys in life, and always lived in fear of one thing or another. They feared the priesthood on one hand, and authority on the other.

May 1, 1960

Propitiation of a jealous and terrible God was the order of the day. Violence, double-dealing, at least chicanery of some sort was another order of the day. That is why Jesus' teachings were so revolutionary. That is why they made such an impact on everyone. A loving God, a merciful One, a forgiving One, was something very difficult to understand.

April 23, 1960

Jesus endeavored to free man of all fears. He set forth a plan for a way of life which would make man conquer all his fears and strengthen his being, so that he could withstand the onslaughts of the influences and forces ever in operation to intimidate and inhibit his activity.

April 26, 1960

Jesus came to teach them kindness and consideration toward others. He taught them that material possessions are as nothing in the spiritual kingdom. Everything there, however, is part of everything here, and there we reap what we have sown here.

October 8, 1955

Scorn of faith and of a belief in God and the spiritual world are as commonplace today as they were in Jesus' day. Sinners are as plentiful, and unrepentant ones are just as many. The only difference is that evil subhuman spirits do not abound as much in and among humanity. Possession of a human body by one of these is rarer, since the human himself has to agree to this phenomenon occurring. The "Dr. Jekyll-Mr. Hyde" thing is based on truth. Fortunately it is extremely rare at this time, since one of Jesus' missions as the perfect manifestation of the Christ was to strengthen mankind's hold on the physical body and make it more difficult for astral beings to contact man.

October 30, 1955

"Whosoever calls to Me for help shall not go unanswered," is the promise of Jesus. Long ages of suffering humanity can testify to the truth of this. Practically all humanity has had some experience in the efficacy of the Christ power at work. Whosoever trusts in the Christ will never be trusting vainly. With Christ, one can have confidence, fortitude, and courage.

January 16, 1948

Jesus taught the solution to problems of life and the methods to raise vibrations to overcome these problems. It is a working philosophy and not an escapist's means.

May 1, 1960

Consider some sayings which have come down to this day and it is surprising how much has survived accurately, although most of Jesus's teachings are lost or hidden in archives. One source of Jesus' teachings is in the archives of Freemasonry, particularly in the Initiations.

April 23, 1960

The basic teachings are disarmingly simple. Old records in many old archives show the basic simplicity of Jesus' teachings as taught by His disciples. Unfortunately, a great deal of it has been swallowed up in ritual, rite and ceremony evolved by the priesthood since time immemorial. Many of these rites have been preserved, almost unchanged, from other religions and have had different labels affixed to them. The simple philosophy taught by Jesus has been amalgamated into the going forms of worship, and the whole mixture was termed Christianity.

Then, again, as things worked out, the reason the teaching took this form was that it could not have reached the different people in any other way because of their level of understanding. Jesus' teachings, to be fully understood, require a very high order of intelligence, a very well disciplined mind, and a tremendous strength of will. This inner strength is practically the most important single factor which must be cultivated in order for man to rid himself of all fears. The fears have their own strength, and man's nature and powers being what they are, the very things man fears he creates and strengthens. Thus, man has a dual work to do. He must cultivate his inner will and strength. Then he must use this inner strength to repel those things and ideas which hamper his regeneration. He must give strength to only those things and ideas which help him attain that kind of life which brings peace, health, and plenty. It is very simple to attain this stage, and Jesus taught how to do it.

April 30, 1960

When Jesus decided to open this school it worried everyone, because no one had any money to do any organizing of anything. But Jesus tackled one thing at a time and somehow it worked out. It seemed miraculous. Frequently the disciples questioned Jesus about some aspect or another when money was needed, and He meditated on it and always came up with a solution. One of the incidents regarding wherewithal is in the Bible, but the story is presented in another guise.

Actually there are several incidents regarding the school in the Bible, but the stories do not mention the school. Frequently the students themselves got involved in the financial difficulties of the school. On the whole, most of the students were poor. Somehow, though, money and means were always found to carry on, and even to prosper. Some students paid urgent bills and were happy to do so. None urged them—they did it on their own. Mothers of some students came as escorts and remained to become students, too. Some pupils had to start from scratch and learn how to read and write. Each who came to the school fitted in, somehow. That was the beauty of the school—everyone seemed to fit in and to make a harmonious whole.

April 29, 1960

At first it was difficult—but word got around and people flocked to the school. At first some people rebelled because there were a few hated Romans in the school, but Jesus made them welcome.

Things were taught by lectures and group discussions. Methods of healing and laws governing life were taught. Many members in the school were women, and there were a couple of teenagers. This was not surprising, because people reached their majority at twelve years of age in those days. On some days' one of the disciples taught classes if Jesus was busy. There were disciples attending as guests, off and on, and they contributed to discussions or offered comments.

There were three different classes in the school. The first was the largest; the second was a little smaller, and the third consisted of the disciples. All the disciples did not attain membership in the last and highest class simultaneously, of course. Some took longer and some shorter periods. Admission to the school was very strict. No one could buy himself or herself into it. The story in the Bible of the young man querying Jesus about becoming a member of the school is true.

Jesus told him to give away everything he had. Only, in the Bible it says that the young man wanted to be a follower. It was more than that. He wanted to become a student. Of course, this was at the time when schools in the black arts were flourishing, too, and openly. But Jesus and his group cut their power. Of course, knowledge of Jesus' school spread rapidly, and that is why crowds followed Him and His followers and disciples wherever He went.

April 30, 1960

In the second year of Jesus' ministry He informed His group of people that they would have a visitor come from far away to give them a lecture. Of course there was a bit of excitement about it. When the day came, everyone turned out in their best in honor of the visitor, and Jesus brought in a man dressed in an exotic costume. Silks and rich cloths covered him. Jewels flashed from his fingers and ears. He had a beautiful smile, was quite dark-skinned, had curly black hair and a short fashioned beard. The stranger spoke through an interpreter, who was Jesus. Jesus introduced the man as His teacher from India. Jesus had spent long years in India and attended mystery schools there.

God looked on humanity that day when Jesus brought the stranger into the school. The man was a tremendously high Initiate, and he came to bless the work of Jesus and His pupils and disciples.

Old books, really manuscripts, describe this visit of one of Jesus' teachers to Palestine. When Jesus was about sixteen years old, one came and took Him to India to study. Actually, He went to Ceylon, an island off the coast of India. Long years were spent to learn the mysteries of being, of nature, of spirit. It was not until almost fourteen years were up that Jesus journeyed back to Egypt to take His final initiations and to start His teachings. All this is contained in manuscripts in the Vatican. Someday these will be published. When Jesus started His school there were only His brothers, one sister, and His mother attending. Gradually He accumulated some ninety people in the three grades. His disciples were the ones who remained through the three grades.

Frequently, when Jesus taught, special topics came up for discussion and Jesus invited guest teachers to speak on their specialties. Thus, this visit of an Indian teacher was not an unusual thing. It was special, though.

May 3, 1960

Jesus brought many innovations to his school. The question and answer period was something entirely new. Experiments in class were another innovation. Word traveled fast and there were more people applying for admission than there was room. There were strict requirements and, through processes of elimination, only those who were really qualified were admitted.

Considering the interest this school created, only those were admitted who could absorb the knowledge which was imparted—and, most importantly—could put it to use.

Usually the classes were taught by the disciples, though guest teachers were not unheard of, as mentioned before. Sometimes pupils were given assignments; and when they were ready with their preparations, they conducted a class. Of course, this was a much sought after opportunity, and a great honor. Its success, as an activity, was because each pupil chosen was best qualified to present the particular topic selected for him. Long hours of preparation were allowed the pupil so that he could adequately present his subject.

Consider the obvious advantage in preparing pupils thus for their later activities as teachers. Jesus followed all activities very closely and sat in on classes presented by the pupils. Everybody knew that it was a great privilege to belong to the school. Needless to say, it was very unpopular with local clergy, who fancied themselves the final authority on matters concerning all types of knowledge.

May 2, 1960

When Jesus saw that his pupils were making good progress, He decided to preach to the populace, too.

October 4, 1955

When Jesus began to teach, He faced the difficulty of making individuals understand Him. To reach them He had to be a storyteller, with tales so simple yet told so that they could not be altered in the retelling. Illiteracy was the order of the day and no one could commit Jesus's sayings in writing. It was over three hundred years later that any of Jesus' exoteric teachings were written down. His stories, after countless retelling, still had the freshness of the original. They carry to this day the hidden message after so many ages have intervened. Generally speaking, humanity accepts what is told and does not delve in depth to verify the New Testament's information. Fortunately, even centuries' flow and countless translations by all kinds of minds did not alter the meaning of the teachings disseminated by Jesus. Grand ideas are ever simple and most simply put.

Although the multitudes did not understand completely the import of the lessons given them, they knew enough to grasp the general essence of the philosophy expounded. And those lessons had practical applications.

"Go ye and do likewise," has an instructor's admonition. The hundreds of people listening understood the teaching without individual wrong interpretation of it.

Many individuals were so impressed that they accepted the teachings and followed them to the letter, unquestioning, unanalytically. But there is far more in the teachings than can be found in the scriptures. The practical application has a grander concept than appears in the Bible, and one must indeed delve deeply to locate it in its fullness and plenitude.

May 2, 1960

Jesus knew His mission was to establish a world religion and understood it to be based on the Hebraic tradition, and He worked at it. Of course, He knew about the Crucifixion. He knew that the cross would be a symbol of His religion, as the pentagram with the point up is the symbol of the new Christianity. Long ages have passed and a few of humanity have progressed beyond the cross and are ready for the pentagram.

The Secret Teachings January 7, 1948

Naturally, the written gospels contain but a small fraction of what Jesus taught. These comprise His teachings to the multitude. Of His teachings to the disciples nothing is said, and it is rightly so, since the multitude was not quickened enough to receive these teachings which are highly esoteric.

Many sought Jesus privately to study the inner meanings; and after Jesus tried them He accepted them, or they dropped out themselves after a few sessions.

Look into the kabbala for some of these teachings, since Jesus, as a Hebrew scholar, was very well acquainted with kabbalistic lore. He also studied with the Egyptians—a remnant of whose lore comprises the teachings of the Rosy Cross Order, and the teachings in the inner ranks of the Jewish religion.

Signs and symbols are very important to master. Their meanings are very important.

January 10, 1948

From the time Jesus started to teach His disciples to the time of His crucifixion, He had over three thousand private pupils who attained illumination.

There were both brothers and sisters whom He taught. In the Bible only an inkling of this is given.

The result of His private teaching was that it has been brought down to this day through secret teachings by individuals who have received it in like manner. Suffice it to say that these teachings have been carried along in an unbroken chain.

October 26, 1955

From every Christian hamlet, estate or palace there goes forth a beam of light whenever the name Christ is mentioned. Far too few people realize the potency of the spoken word. Perhaps if they did, there would be more controlled thinking in the world today. Far too few practice the religion Jesus taught, both to the multitudes and behind closed and tiled doors. He imparted the inner secret teachings to those who would found the priesthood. Their teaching held the occult significance and explanation of the outer, exoteric teaching. Even today few realize that the New Testament does not contain all of Jesus' teachings. In spite of many references in the text itself of the New Testament to the fact that Jesus taught His disciples in secret and that He taught many more things than He spoke of in public, today most of the people honestly feel that the whole substance of Jesus' teachings is given in the New Testament.

The fact of the matter is that this is not true. The reference in Acts to the hundred and twenty of the inner group who met in an upper room after Jesus' crucifixion tells at least that there was an inner group. Further than that there is nothing—not even a hint—to indicate what comprised the secret teachings. The wonder is that more people have not questioned it or made an effort to find out for themselves. It is only logical to reason that it would be of little import for a Son of God to come into incarnation and not leave more then He did. His miracles are described, but the method of them is not given in the Bible.

It is true that Christian Science teaches a method of realization, but it does not teach—and can never teach with the limited resources it has—the full power of the Christ force which can literally lift a mountain and cast it into the sea. It does not teach the occult significance of statements in the Bible. It teaches nothing of the power of breath. Lastly, it does not teach how natural laws operate in the performance of miracles.

Yes, there are miracles done every day. Only, they are not miraculous when one understands the laws in operation which brought them about.

There is a sight beyond normal human sight; there is a hearing, smell, and so on with all the senses, which are attributes of the spiritual body man has. Man is both physical and spiritual. What happens to the physical is a direct effect of what happens in the spiritual. And Jesus taught everything that pertained to the spiritual body.

January 8, 1948

That is how Jesus taught. To the multitudes He taught great truths in simple language. To His disciples He taught secret mystical truths which gave them great power. He also transmitted some of His own powers to them by touching them. That is how He raised their vibrations.

May 11, 1960

When Jesus taught His disciples He warned them to refrain from interpolating their own thinking into His teachings, which might result in the meaning becoming lies. Unwittingly, teachings get twisted until they lose their rightful meanings.

April 25, 1960

And God spoke to the disciples and exhorted them to follow the dictates of Jesus. Each disciple, in the recesses of his own heart, knew that he must follow Jesus even unto the end. And thus it was. Each disciple was taught according to his own temperament and Sun sign so that he might be able to reach his own vibrationally compatible learner. With a little study perhaps you could work out which disciple corresponds to which Sun sign. And there were twelve men. Each disciple, in fact, revealed a higher and a lower aspect of his nature, which in turn reveals that he presented both aspects and also the manner of their manifesting. One defaulted, since he did not have a higher aspect in his makeup. And one came later to replace him. Each disciple was fulfilling a requirement, a role for which he was suited. Of course there were the four apostles of the Gospels, and a further study should point out to which sign each apostle corresponded.

The only drawback to this is that it would take a tremendous amount of research, because so little is known regarding some disciples. It is only the principal ones who received the most attention. Some lesser disciples tagged after the ones with whom they were in sympathy.

Each disciple understood only as much of the teachings as his understanding could fathom. But he was an instrument of the Almighty and fulfilled his role. When new manuscripts become known, much the disciples' work will be revealed.

April 23, 1960

When Jesus was on Earth He undertook a tremendous task. This task enabled Him to reach as many people as possible in the short span of His activity. Really, His work consisted of learning as well as teaching, for one can only teach what one has learned, so that the truth regarding man's sojourn in this world would have some meaning. Eventually, man extricates himself from the illusory life in matter, but Jesus taught the method by which the process could be shortened considerably.

Influences particular to matter are always at work endeavoring to interfere with man's progress in his regeneration process. However, man in his blind blundering way still triumphs eventually in one way or another. Think well on why and wherefore it was necessary for Jesus to show humanity why it should concentrate on leading a particular type of life to survive and make progress. Fortunately, man can judge for himself in his own particular outlook (and this outlook is not possessed by animals) as to the validity of Jesus' teachings. The marvel of Jesus' teachings is that they reached the twelve basic types of people.

Yes, there are twelve basic types of people manifesting on Earth. That was the reason there were twelve disciples. Each disciple had to have special training by Jesus to be able to reach his own type of person. This makes sense, does it not?

There was a tremendous plan in Jesus' mind, given Him by God, to put into effect to hasten man's regeneration and awaken him to a sense of reality, which unfortunately is not the outward sense-life that man is experiencing when he lives in the flesh on the three-dimensional plane.

April 23, 1960

Each disciple underwent very rigorous training, according to his own nature and temperament and also understanding; so that he could be able to reach and present from his own viewpoint a plan of living, thinking, and being which would make it understandable to his own kind of people.

April 27, 1960

It is necessary to love much to conquer fear. Jesus loved much to be able to devote his whole life to humanity and give it up for them. Probably the next best thing any of His disciples could do, was to devote all their efforts to propagating the teachings. As the teachings spread, however, all kinds of extraneous information were added and the original teachings were twisted to suit the preachers of the moment. Then there was always an honest misunderstanding about certain points. It was all work of mouth initially, and there was not enough acumen or understanding to fathom the abstract aspect of Jesus' teachings. Jesus was a very learned man, having studied in mystery schools of India and having traveled extensively. There is much said about His not having left any written records but that all of his teachings were verbal. This is partly true. His innermost teachings, and teachings to the populace were verbal. There are teachings which are never committed to paper. These can be communicated only by word of mouth. The reason is twofold. These things give power. Power cannot be misused, even in ignorance. The speeches and preaching to the populace were spontaneous things to fit the occasion. But Jesus did write extensively. Some of His writings have been suppressed intentionally to keep up the myth that Jesus' work was all oral.

October 4, 1955

Gradually, as the central philosophy and the basic principles underlying Jesus' teachings evolved in the people's minds, groups gathered and formed a more or less permanent church, as it were. These people were not in any way the Ecclesiastes of the day—far from it. They were simple folk who did not find the answer to their problems in the faiths of the day and turned to Christianity, which had the power to touch off the imagination. Especially so when the ones preaching Jesus' gospel were such fanatic zealots.

And that brings us to the phenomenon which has never been equaled in the history of the world, that is, the fanaticism which swept through the people when Christianity was in its infancy. It was fantastic. People bled and died, exulting at the privilege of bleeding and dying in the name of Christ. The force and power of it impressed all the so-called pagans and converted many. It was a highly emotional religion. This element has not departed from it entirely, even to this day, and manifests in some sects as a form of fervent hysteria.

Of course, those whose souls are highly evolved, and the Christ is manifesting in full strength in them, will never resort to shouting and dancing, shrieking and breast-beating, handling of venomous serpents, or otherwise behaving like hysterical adolescents. One who manifests the Christ force will always be calm, quiet, soft-spoken, and in full possession of his emotional controlling factor. He will be dignified without being proud. In fact, his mien will be humble with that humbleness which bespeaks true nobility.

April 20, 1960

When Peter established the old church in Rome, some people expected Christ to appear immediately. Some priests even preached the momentary reappearance of Him who had been crucified. There was that constant air of expectancy. And that was the way it continued through the years in the Christian world. Everyone was waiting for the reappearance of Jesus. Understand, this state of affairs was necessary to establish a church among the barbaric, semi-civilized Europeans.

Chapter Three

Religion

March 30, 1963

Man belongs to the animal kingdom until he becomes a true human having a soul consciousness. Every human has a soul, it is true, but very few have soul consciousness. People are asleep, as it were—not aware that they have a spiritual aspect of life. This is where religion comes in. Something is needed to keep the truth of his being before him.

All religions are basically the same. The purpose of each is to make man soul-conscious to fulfill his purpose in being born.

November 10, 1955

Approbation of self is useless unless one can gain insight into circumstances and their causes. As one evaluates self correctly, to that degree is one evolved. Self-satisfaction is bad, because it hinders progress so necessary to launch forth into conscious effort for integration with God. Whatever experience's one has, they try and test the individual. Gain can be had from using resources within oneself which will point out the way to go.

November 10, 1955

There is no man or woman alive that at some period in his or her life, has not asked what is in back of religion. Who is God? What scheme promulgated the laws set forth in the Ten Commandments, the Sermon on the Mount, and in the writings of philosophers who left rules of conduct to men in order for them to reach heaven? What and where is heaven?

We are assured that heaven is a state of being and that the kingdom of heaven is within one's own being. And the laws set forth the how of reaching that kingdom of heaven within one's own being. If we follow the laws, we are supposed to achieve the kingdom of heaven in which we attain everlasting conscious life.

March 26, 1948

"God in heaven" is a peculiar expression. It is very revealing when analyzed. Heaven, of course, is a state of being. Although there are, at various heights above the surface of the Earth, locations where souls of various vibrations congregate—and the higher the soul's rate of vibration, the higher it will be found—of these heavens we are not speaking. The "heaven" we wish to speak of lies within the heart of each individual, wherein dwells the consciousness of God.

November 10, 1955

The everlasting conscious life aspect is stressed by every religious movement and is the reason for striving to attain the kingdom of heaven. As we look about us, we see life as manifested on Earth—life with its cycles of birth, growth and decay—and the idea of everlasting life does not enter physical manifestation. It is true enough that the seed carries on the particular life of the species from which it emanated. However, we are considering now the human individual self-conscious everlasting life.

It is apparent at once that everlasting life does not mean continuous living on this plane of material manifestation. Therefore, how does it tie in with the physical within which is the abode of the kingdom of heaven in which everlasting conscious life has its place?

Inside, somewhere within our bodies, lies a point which can guarantee everlasting life if that point is contacted.

As we read all the laws set forth by the various scriptures of religious movements, we see that each shows a Way. Also, we see that there is a similarity between the laws. If analyzed thoroughly, they are alike.

Upon examining a human being, a living one, we find that he emanates warmth and something else. He emanates a kind of magnetic force. We can prove this by our senses. We may be alone in a room; but when someone comes in we will know it. We may not see him or hear him, but eventually, depending upon how sensitive we are, we feel that we are not alone.

What made us feel the presence of someone else? He emanated a force or energy which we intercepted as they undulated from him, much like waves. To prove that you emanate a strong force, as does everyone else, you may shake hands with others and watch for reactions. To some, you will be attracted; and by some, you will be repelled. Study will confirm the laws of attraction and repulsion governing magnetism. A human's magnetism can also affect matter.

The generator of this magnetism is the sum of the forces emanating from the seven gyrating centers within the human body. Find the working secrets of these seven centers and you will find everlasting conscious life.

To find one's place in the scheme of things takes much study and evaluation of self. It can be done with deep meditation.

January 23, 1948

Far-reaching results are obtained when man gives himself wholly to living by the voice within. Then God can act directly through him. Formerly, all men knew of no other nomenclature for this phenomenon than that of conscience. But now man has advanced sufficiently to know that it is the Voice of God speaking and directing to do His will.

March 30, 1963

As soon as man can begin to sense his own everlastingness, or that aspect of himself which is everlasting, then he is on his way. At long last he contacts his soul. And when he contacts his own soul, that contact becomes cosmic consciousness. The soul is the point of contact. Man requires this contact with his soul to be the Master of all, which he indeed is supposed to be.

January 23, 1948

It devolves on only a small handful of people, comparatively speaking, to raise the comprehension and knowledge of humanity.

The greatest step is to make a human aware of a Being, or rather the existence of the First Cause Creator. When he achieves a knowledge of and faith in the All Good, from there all is simple. This is the hardest hurdle.

Once a human has that questioning, vaguely terrifying sensation as to his beginning and ultimate achievement, he will seek the answer. Material wealth and success will lose their savor and will fail to appease that craving for the eternal life which is every human's heritage, if he will but take it.

Many human souls achieve that knowledge only through suffering, and that is why there is so much misery on Earth. Too many people would become too lazy to progress if they were happy. Naturally, all unhappiness is created by themselves alone, because they listen to the dictates of their puny material brain instead of to the All Knowing voice within, which always knows best. Long familiarity with the process of listening to the voice within, creates a life of tranquility, sureness of self, and the ability to do the right thing at the right time. So few, so very few can really do this.

Mental images are important. Be careful to explain only to the right people the great power of creating in that media. That process has functioned from the beginning. The all-important task is to start the quest for God in every human on Earth.

August 15, 1966

It is understandable why there is no God for some people. God consciousness requires a refined type of awareness which animal man can gradually attune to beyond the limitations of his objective sense perceptions.

We cannot, of course, belittle the tremendous mechanism of the objective body. After all, it is the only means by which man can become a real human and be "reborn," as it were.

The key to a realization of God is desire, a desire to be one with God, so intensely that it encompasses the combined force of love, despair, immolation. This desire cannot be a "sometime" thing. An hour or so Sunday is not enough. An hour or so each day is not enough. It must become one's whole life. Each moment it must be sustained, and the intensity must be kept up—increased, if possible. Who can achieve it? There were some who did. There are some who do. An intellectual inquiry into the possible existence of a Prime Mover transcending anything comprehensible to the physical mind is useless for attunement (at-one-ment) with God.

The body is a receiving set which has to be tuned up to an extremely high frequency. And not all bodies have that capability. The body has to be refined first, and all elements lowering its frequency have to be eliminated.

The Ten Commandments are a good start. The Sermon on the Mount follows. The Eightfold Path is another way. The signposts to God are there if one wants to make the journey. Whatever method one uses, it serves to eliminate the interference in the circuit of the body.

In other words, one cleans out the Augean stables, which is the physical body.

What will you make of yourself? A Tzaddik, a Buddha, a Christ-ian? It does not matter what tag you wear. The important thing is that you are a pilgrim on the way to reach God consciousness.

What is the single outstanding deterrent to the stupendous task of transforming oneself into a true human being? It is fear.

The paramount category of fear is that of being ridiculed. Many other aspects can be fear of arousing animosity, and also ostracism, and all the way to that of exploring the fearsome darkness in the core of one's own being. None but the strong-willed dare venture down into those Stygian depths of utter despairing aloneness and stripped-nakedness of the ego.

All learning, all imposed knowledge communicated by the physical senses is left at the portals of the physical sense mechanism as one wilfully steps over the brink into the depths of the real self within and faces that which one really is.

To those who have questioned the meaning and purpose of life from time immemorial—to those is communication mandatory. Release of the real human being enslaved in animal man becomes a single-pointed purpose and the true achievement of a lifetime.

The reward is conscious immortality.

Immortality October-December 1939

Consider the question of an individual's immortality. Religion teaches that each individual has an immortal soul. But religious teachings are so shrouded in allegories and vague allusions to the truth that it is difficult to comprehend fully exactly what is being taught. That is why there are as many understandings as there are individuals.

The whole sum of religious teachings as you know it is that the personality is the immortal part. It is taught that a new soul is created to tenant each newly born body. This does not happen to be the truth.

The spiral, ever widening, the gyration that governs all matter, is applied to human birth and to every type of manifestation. Why are some individuals more gifted than others? Why are the mental capacities of some individuals in one family greater than in the other members of the same family? Both have a like background and heritage. The experience and knowledge must have been acquired somewhere, somehow. This thought has been voiced as far back as thought exists.

The Egyptians had it worked out in a very elaborate system. According to them, as long as any trace of a body exists, the soul could not inhabit another body. They prognosticated a very dark age for humanity and instituted a method of mummification which held them back from incarnating for several succeeding thousands of years.

In the Apostle's Creed is contained the ending "I believe…in the resurrection of the body and life everlasting. Amen." This refers to rebirth and not to some wholesale resurrection of the body at some Judgment Day, in some future age.

April 14, 1960

God gave each human soul a memory and the ability to carry on accomplishments from life to life.

January 21, 1948

The lesson of reincarnation is this. There is no inflexible rule about it. Some on Earth are truly souls reincarnating periodically. Other souls have taken bodies for doing a particular kind of work. Some have only one life and proceed onward. Reincarnation is an exception rather than the rule.

Nevertheless, there are millions upon millions of souls who are reincarnating regularly. It is getting to be a rule rather than an exception. It is not such a good practice because it cuts down on the Creator's harvest of souls, and sometimes retards an individual's growth.

December 31, 1960

Now consider what people have been searching for these many millennia which could prove the continuity of life in all phases of existence. The proof they lack is in their own minds. They have to develop their minds to the point where they can gain the awareness of things as they are. Forbid the thought that it will lead to a further materiality. As the mind is refined and the activity of the physical brain quickens, people will naturally develop the necessary awareness of the reality and truth of everything. Right now, everything is accepted on faith, because most people trust another's veracity in reporting the truth. But the time is coming when all will be known by every individual. As a whole people are beginning to gradually awaken to this fact and are becoming aware, themselves, that something lies beyond the area of the testimony of their five receptor senses. There is a realm of the mind beyond the physical senses which is vastly richer and truer than anything one can see, hear, feel, smell, or taste. And the beauty of it is that it is possible to bring things into physical manifestation with the proper application of the mind. Naturally, advanced souls have known this since the beginning of time, but the level of consciousness has to rise in all of humanity until an average mean is reached before one can introduce something or some new idea.

Mysticism January 1, 1948

Living under varying conditions develops a person through varying rates of speed in his vibrations. Sometimes in one life an individual may speed through all three degrees because a good foundation was laid in the previous several lives.

Given enough peace and quiet for meditation and time for reading, an individual will raise his vibrations in spite of himself. A life of priesthood will do wonders if the individual does not develop an avarice for money. Caring for the development of the souls in the folds of a church and a constant application of God's laws to one's daily living has created many an unconscious Master.

Some have become frightened when they started seeing thought forms and hearing higher vibrations that are not usually perceptible to human ears, and have willfully shut their minds to these manifestations of their own higher rates of vibration. Doubtless these uninformed individuals thought they were losing their minds, when in reality they were regaining once-lost faculties.

When this happens, in the succeeding life the individual will be born into surroundings which will enable him to study mysticism under guidance. The initiations into higher spheres of comprehension will be conscious, and fearless. And it is right that this should be so, because an unguided individual can cause much harm through his ignorance, but this ignorance will not stop the effects of his actions from taking place.

If the individual is persistent enough, a teacher is sent to him or he is taken out of his environment and put into another, more conducive to his quest. God knows His own workers, whether in the flesh or not. These workers have been so ordained from the beginning. They always lead, whether it is in a family, a group, or a nation. In many ways, do they do so. No matter what form of expression they use, it always raises the vibration of the soul-personality within the ones in their sphere of influence. Great Souls invariably help these individuals if allowed to do so.

January 1, 1961

It is still largely a mystery to man how the process of evolvement works. In these past few decades' man has penetrated only the frontiers of the eternal mysteries. Most of the truths are still hidden. However, they will not always be hidden, because man will not always remain the dense clod that he is. He will develop powers of perception, understanding, and ability of which he has not yet even dreamed. He will truly be Godlike, even as it is his destiny to be. That was what he was created for, in truth.

Only those who desire with their whole hearts a union with God, are raising their vibrations sufficiently to attract aid from the Invisible Hosts of Teachers and Helpers. Persons living without aspirations betray their heritage.

August 13, 1966

Will is striving.

Spiritual knowledge is the highest and innermost faculty of knowledge. It is independent of any form, either sensual or mental. It can penetrate to the imperishable essence of things.

Scientific materialists do not recognize the nature of God; nor do they understand themselves and the world in relation to God. This type of understanding has its seat in the heart, where love and knowledge coincide. True love is a kind of knowledge and spirit is loving: both have fundamentally one goal, which is infinity.

January 20, 1948

Many souls struggle to know God, but others speak not of Him, so that it is too much of a closed subject. More people every day should talk more about Him and bring Him into their conversation. Each time they do so it opens the door for an outpouring of Divine Love. That is Inspiration! Let us all pray for God's guidance. Many souls, through lack of knowledge, confuse Christ with God. Christ is the force which is an attribute of the Great Source, and it is through this force that we can attain admittance into the everlasting kingdom. Living according to the laws as set forth in the Sermon on the Mount is the key to that kingdom. It matters not of what creed, faith or understanding one is.

January 1, 1961

One who calls above and dreads worldly aspirations will consider eternal life. Therefore, call upon Christly light for illumination.

A Primer of Mysticism:

The first requisite is an earnest heartfelt desire, a yearning for betterment of self in some way. There is a dissatisfaction with one's life and a knowledge deep within one's consciousness that somewhere, somehow one can change it all. This becomes a prayer for betterment of self and the conditions around one. In due time, perception sharpens and one becomes aware of things around one which have existed all along, but one was always too busy or preoccupied to notice them.

Following this awareness comes detachment as an attribute of the seeker, and he can view everything from a perspective he lacked before. He now weighs and organizes the facts he sees, hears, tastes, feels, and smells. Thus, he becomes more completely a person. Also, he increases his capacity for suffering and also for joy.

Prayer will become a regular practice. But prayer will change its form. Instead of words, the prayer will become a meditation upon some phase of existence, or of a manifestation for which the individual will seek to know the meaning.

When the individual attains detachment, he will realize the futility of greed for power, possessions and fame merely for self-satisfaction. The individual will see in others what greed has wrought. The signs will have been visible all along, but the individual had not the awareness to see them for what they were.

The faculty of the realization and perception of truth through the senses will enable the individual to evaluate correctly everybody and everything which affects him. In that way, he will live his life for the best advantage to himself and his neighbors. He will daily feel more at one with the God of his heart.

Should one deny self the pleasures of life? Is it detrimental to inner growth to heed the calls of the flesh? Is it necessary to deny oneself a normal life or to retire from the affairs of the world to lead the life of return to God?

All these questions crowd in, one on top of the other. It is just these questions and teachings of past ages which have kept man from leading a godly life. A veil of fear has been thrown between the human and God. This fear is part of an elaborate system of Churchianity which battens itself on the credulity and ignorance of the masses of humanity. Its half-truths hold individuals chained to the block or pedestal of its powerful organization. The so-called fear of hellfire and damnation is a lie. This elaborate system of various types of sin is a lie, too. The truth of the matter is that sin is a breaking of a law which throws a person's scheme of living off balance which he has to correct by making up on the other side to make the balance even again. That is all there is to it. And no one can remit or forgive that imbalance in a person's life. He himself has to attend to it.

The Blood of the Lamb, the Crucifixion, and the washing away of sins cannot remit or forgive that unbalance in a person's life. He himself has to do it.

In other words, the Blood of the Lamb, the Crucifixion, and the washing away of the sins of the world pertains to something entirely different which is of deep metaphysical concept, and does not refer to the sinning of the ordinary mortal.

The sins of the everyday man are his lessons and means of gaining experience. He has learned through countless ages the folly of abuse of his own person and also the persons of others. Every time he breaks one of the Ten Commandments (which are definite laws operating in the universe), he sets the machinery in motion which will make up for it. In time, if not immediately, he suffers the consequences of his actions.

Of course, this balancing is constantly working with the good, and also the evil an individual does. A curious law in this operation is that the effects are always tenfold.

Laws for living to preserve an even balance are plainly set forth in the Ten Commandments. These cannot be improved upon. Every mortal on Earth can follow them and will not live uncomfortably. When an individual is ready to live an entirely Christly existence, he then follows the Sermon on the Mount.

In this primer we will examine the whys of the Commandments. "I Am the Lord thy God. Thou shalt have no other Gods before Me." "I Am" is the key to this commandment. What is this "I Am?" Volumes have been written on these two words. The greatest minds in history have pondered on these, even as they will continue pondering into posterity.

Yet it is one of the easiest to understand. It does not refer to "somebody up there," but it refers to you, yourself. Every time you say "I Am" you proclaim yourself Lord. Understand, this does not mean the physical part of you, because that part is only a manifestation, but it is that part of you with which you will try to establish contact on your voyage into mysticism.

Let us examine this matter further. Of course you realize that there is some sort of order in the universe. If you study chemistry, physics, in fact anything, you will learn a lot about these laws governing action and reaction. Then you will realize that there is a Cause, a Prime Mover, involved.

This applies to the universe and to everything contained in it. There is a Cause which started this manifestation of an orderly universe. For want of a better name, people named it God. In reality, it should not be named, because it is too vast and incomprehensible for the mind of man to fathom. All we know and can understand are the manifestations which are wonderful and breathtaking when we stop to contemplate them. And we do not have to go far afield with telescopes or microscopes to find the laws operating in due order according to their nature. Merely looking around attentively at everything and everyone will be sufficient.

The thing which will be evident is that the laws are operating because of an Intelligent Cause.

Another thing which we will notice is that the human being is the highest form of manifestation on the Earth, as is apparent to our material physical senses. Furthermore, this is because man is self-conscious. Oh, yes, other things are conscious, too: animals, plants, even minerals and rocks (in which atoms whirl as in everything else); but only man is self-conscious. He is truly a microcosm of the vast macrocosm. He is indeed a unique being, because he has a mind with which he can bring into manifestation ideas from the plane of thought. He is a creator on a microcosmic scale, as compared with the creation of the universe.

That mind part of himself we have become accustomed to calling soul. And when we realize that our bodies are temples for our souls we will cease abusing them and will make them real servants of the soul.

The power of the soul is so great that it is awesome to realize it. It knows everything: past, present, and future. It can make anything possible. Once the mind has established conscious contact with the soul, there are no mysteries.

Countless mystics have proved this since time immemorial.

And the rest of the commandments are the precepts to follow, without compromise, in order for the physical mind to establish contact with the soul.

January 13, 1948

Generations of men learn and study and meditate upon a subject which is in its essence very simple and build up a complicated system of philosophy about it. Thus, theology has its sway. The results of physical brain activity ever explain what intuition renders in a flash. This merely fulfills the process ordained by God. Out of simplicity into complexity is the process.

Find a mean, or middle of each subject, to arrive at the truth concerning it.

Take the law, "Thou shalt not steal," for instance. The law is simple. To arrive at its reason one must go to the spiritual man. Every object taken which is not earned becomes attached to the immaterial man. When one sees psychically a thief, he looks like a peddler with a mountain of things he must carry. The law is such that every one of those objects must be returned ere the spiritual man can attain illumination.

August 16, 1960

Things of the spirit are more often best appreciated in a spirit of honest inner enjoyment.

Once thoughts are under control, then "renunciation of will" takes place. An erroneous conception of this does a great deal of harm. Most individuals, well-meaning ones who interpret this phrase wrongly, become meek and cringing, breathlessly rushing around doing the will of others. That is wrong. When it is said, "...Thy will be done...," it means God's will, and not the will of everybody else. Renunciation of will means learning to listen to "God's Voice within." Oh, yes, it is there, but we are all too busy rushing around doing our or others' wills and letting our thoughts dart around like thousands of minnows in a shallow pond. We literally drown out that "Still Small Voice" which is always there if we will but still the clamor in our hearts and listen.

As the aspirant lives more and more in the spirit, he spiritualizes his physical self and his head shines like a lighted candle. The old paintings of saints with halos are no invention. It is really true. Some halos extend for miles, and the colors are beautiful.

September 15, 1959

God prepared a way for mankind to ascend unto Himself. The paths are many, but the final one has all the others leading into it. Great honors await the one who achieves this absorption. To be absorbed—yet retain individuality and identity—is a great mystery beyond man's comprehension. It is all accomplished by the power of the mind. Where there is proper meditation and concentration, the faculties develop, which makes for spiritual growth.

December 16, 1947

Man should know he will attain sainthood. Men lead different lives but attain the same ends. This is true because each has a different pattern to weave. Like snow, the flakes are all different, no two being alike, yet it is still snow. God knows which ones are His Chosen Ones, not through His own choice, but through that knowledge of soul in man which tells Him of man's own choice. When a soul consciously lets it be known that it will work with Christ, there is everything possible done to help this soul. Punishment, sorrow, the suffering which in people's minds is synonymous with living in Christ, is not true.

August 22, 1950

God brings happiness to all who turn to Him. Many think that the path to good is one of sorrow and privation. That is not necessarily so. One treading the Path should be healthy, wealthy and wise, and have peace, joy and contentment. This is the way that the New Dispensation brings to the Western world.

August 11, 1961

God brings his children to fruitful lands, not to barren wastes. Evil influences put further restrictions on humanity. The more freedom one has the greater is the freedom to evolve.

December 16, 1947

Living in Christ is a joyous experience. When a man or woman resolves to live right and give a tenth of his worldly income to the furtherance of good works, from that day his life will change for the better. Out of nowhere, seemingly normal occurrences will transform his or her mode of life to a higher and better one. This is a truth that is everlastingly in operation. But many a hand which reaches forth for that cup—which the individual has to drain to the last drop—trembles, and many a man cringes from the expected bitter brew, only to find in that cup the sweetest wine of creation.

Living in Christ is not a restricting experience. On the contrary, it is a full, rich experience. It opens the wealth of all planes and leaves them at the disposal of the individual. Wealth of thought and wealth of material possessions all comes to man. The only thing in the world that man has to do is say, "Christ, come and run my life as it should go." Then, listen to the Christ within the heart and do, say, or think that which He says. That is the meaning of the saying concerning the casting of one's burden on the Lord. Instead of it being a hard and sorrowful life as is the popular conception, it becomes a wonderfully joyous one, with all opportunities available and at one's disposal. What if the Christ within forbids the following of a certain pleasure which the body has been inured to? For every pleasure given up, there will be another one given, which will be ten times more enjoyable and, what is more, not harmful to the body. That is a truth which cannot be repeated often enough.

January 2, 1948

Only the pure in heart can know God. Cleansing the heart is the first requisite of any individual desiring eternal union with God. Cleansing the heart consists of adoption of all virtues. Then nothing detrimental to his spiritual growth will find room to lodge in the heart.

The heart is the center of spiritual man. Whoever receives the seed of Christ into his heart and allows it to grow will know and realize that spiritual growth starts in the heart and not in the head. When the spiritual man is full grown, his point of communication will be through a point inside his head.

Love is the only emotion having its origin in the heart. Individuals naturally point to the heart when they speak of love. The symbol of love is a heart. That explains why love is a necessary adjunct of spiritual growth.

Untold glories are awards of a fully developed spiritual man. The school of Earth is a hard one, but the results make it worth while to put up with all sorts of conditions. Each experience contributes its rate of vibration to the individual.

March 21, 1948

Meeting of souls in matrimony can either be of great benefit to both or of great detriment to both. A joining together can raise the vibrations or plunge both souls deeper into materiality. Love, even physical love, is the greatest factor in bringing humanity back to God.

Filling the cup of joy can be accomplished more easily by love. Love is the heritage of every human. If a life is loveless it is because the individual has excluded it consciously.

Forlornness is a material emotion entirely. It lessens the vibrations automatically.

February 25, 1949

Many speak of studying mysticism later in life. When a person starts saying this, it means that he will be ready to study in his next incarnation. The body requires an adequate brain to cope with abstractions. The brain is specially constructed to do this. There are only a few brains which have this faculty fully developed. What the body requires is the whip of necessity, as it were, which drives the individual to try to provide for it. Only the truly great and fully equipped souls can bring an existence into being requiring less and less effort. They can draw from the cosmic and bring into being enough to provide for needs. This is a special kind of ability requiring a special kind of concentration and a determination to provide a wholesome existence.

If opulence follows, it is because the soul in incarnation deserves it and has earned it.

March 17, 1949

When a soul longs for union with God, a means is always provided. When an individual has a life with which he is not satisfied, that is because he must seek a means for communion with God. However, there is such a thing as ordering one's life to provide the means, too.

February 16, 1949

When many have brought sorrow to an individual, he finally learns not to go to others like himself, but to turn to God. It is true that an individual turns to God as a last resort.

Prayer June 5, 1948

We grow in knowledge and intuition as we apply ourselves to contemplation and study of things regarding our souls. Many souls advance great strides during one life, while others repeat the same experiences in life after life, because they lack initiative to seek new experiences and knowledge. Rarely does a human leap from one extreme into another.

Prayer is the most wonderful help in the soul's progress.

November 9, 1954

Beseech the heavenly powers to aid thee in the comprehension of Divine Law which affects certain things regarding results of actions you wish to be obviated. Any result can be nullified if need be; but one must understand the law and not break it, however work according to it.

November 2, 1954

How can Christ deliver one from dishonor and disgrace? He will help one in answer to fervent, ardent prayer, self-abnegation and fasting. All efforts bent toward Him, pointing to one desire, flow straight to Him for consideration.

Believe and it shall be done according to your belief.

February 15, 1949

Some pray for worldly goods, others pray for success, and a very few pray for better conditions for humanity. There is a selfishness of one sort or another always connected with these prayers. It would be a calamity if all the prayers were always answered. Even man, himself, changes his mind from day to day as to his wants. When he wishes to have something, he prays and works for it. Later he realizes that the object of his desires is not the necessity of his life at all.

November 10, 1955

Christ knows everyone's need, and that is not just a generality. Anyone calling to Christ will have his aura examined by the Christ's hosts of Invisible Helpers and such aid will be given as is needed to evolve nearer to God. No one cries in vain. All are helped. Perhaps the help is not in the manner expected. Nevertheless, all are helped in the best and wisest way.

February 15, 1949

There is a constant stream of strong lines of force comprising these prayers and petitions being launched into the cosmic. The streams fill the desire world with their patterns of beauty and horribleness. The cosmic sift these requests and laws of nature determine which requests are granted and which are not. No thought, no wish, no longing, no harmful invective but has its counterpart in the cosmic, and can benefit or harm. Mankind must protest itself from this web of destiny which others are spinning and into which an individual may stumble unwittingly and become enmeshed.

April 17, 1948

A Prayer: Salvation of Humanity, come to our aid. Lead us to that cosmic consciousness where humanity will know what laws to obey and follow for the greatest good of all. Many Great Souls have sacrificed themselves to come and teach humanity the laws governing attainment of Thy cosmic consciousness. O Greatest Salvation, Thou art unmanifest on this earthly plane, and never can manifest, but Thou can send Thy all-powerful influence to save poor humanity before the final dissolution of the Earth. Man is hastening this process, through his wickedness: Save him, Thou All-Powerful, Thou Final Authority from whom all proceeds. Send that ray which opens men's minds to others' thoughts. When nothing is hid, all things will rise higher in vibration. All too few have raised their consciousness to that ray, which does not touch the Earth because the Earth is not of the blessed. Prayer is all too self-engrossed by the greatest number of humanity to raise them into contact with that ray. Direct that ray, Thou All-Good, to this troubled Earth. It is the only thing that can save poor man, and he will attempt to shine the brightest when all can see his emanations. CHI RHO!

Angels January 21, 1948

Angels are beings doing a special kind of work on Earth by special permission. They help humanity as best they can and instruct the soul when a human is asleep. One of their important tasks is not to allow souls to remain on the earth plane after they have cast off their bodies. There are means of education on the cosmic plane to which the soul is taken.

October-December 1939

Lesser powers proceed from God. Christians term them beings of the angelic kingdom. This kingdom is parallel to the human kingdom. It, however, does not contain the earth element. There are also collective spirits of races, of the animal kingdom, and of plant life. The gods of the ancient Greeks, Romans, and Egyptians are not figments of imagination. The ancients all knew about collective spirits. A good example of a race spirit is Jehovah (or Yah Veh) of the Old Testament. A modern manifestation of a race spirit gone amok is the German one. Hitler claims to be in communication with it. Moses certainly was in communication with a race spirit when he received the decalogue.

The existence of a race spirit is very real. It is the sum total of its people's thoughts, emotions, ambitions, loves, hatreds, wills, ideas and ideals.

May 29, 1949

Angels watch over humanity unceasingly. They bring all hope and encouragement to an erring humanity, and as much help as humanity will avail itself of and use.

God blesses those who open their hearts to Him and allow His Wisdom to flow unhampered through their beings.

Follow precepts as set forth in all great scriptures, according to your faith and understanding, whereupon salvation will surely come.

April 19, 1948

The cultivation of mentality belongs to the sphere of a particular set of forces which we call angels, although that is an inadequate description of these entities. They consciously assume positions near the individual and play their forces through him. This stimulates his brain cells to greater activity and speeds up the vibration of an individual as a whole. Conversely, the Hierarchical Helpers take another individual into their special care and shield him from unnecessary annoyances, allowing only such as build for strength, or provide a peaceful life if the individual requires such for a steady development.

March 28, 1948

Angels are working with humanity constantly. When they see a Master through whom they can communicate who can help them, there is great rejoicing. These angels help the Master as much as, if not more than he helps them.

January 26, 1948

When man fares forth into the world he has guardians to help him. These inspire him to learn everything he should know concerning his progress. Rules of right living are plentiful to lead man onto the right path.

Nonaggression is perhaps one of the first essentials to a good life. A man, to advance spiritually, must forget self sufficiently so that he can live at peace with his neighbors.

Man's angel guides try to inspire him like this. Frequently, it is necessary to allow the human to suffer so that he may learn the error of his ways.

However, a direct inflow of great spiritual light will accomplish this end, as well. Yes, a man is always under guidance and inspiration.

March 7, 1948

God leads all toward presence in His domain. Growth, expansion, and knowledge are all given man so that he will comprehend all the arithmetical, mathematical and geometrical shapes of the universe. Given every help and assistance, man plows ahead, unknowing, uncomprehending and not caring that he is watched over constantly.

Angels give thousands of years of service in this loving task.

Occasionally a man will lift his forehead to the sky and call to God and yearn toward His kingdom. And the angels rejoice.

March 27, 1949

How can glorious angels give material things? Impossible. What they can and do give are spiritual treasures which are everlasting.

Churchianity November 7, 1954

People are prone to believe the letter of everything they read. They place particular credulity on the printed word. If it is printed, it must be true, they argue. When a point is to be verified, they rush for the printed word to find it, never stopping to reason that it may be merely another man's opinion. And the other man may be entirely wrong. The same may be said of the many, many different biographies of Jesus. Somewhere the truth exists.

March 15, 1948

So-called religions are merely the elaborated teachings of ordinary individuals. Their convictions were so strong that they could sway others to their way of thinking, who in turn influenced others, and so on.

The universal truth is very simple: there is but one God, and a Hierarchy which rule the world which should be obeyed but not worshiped. Each great man who set forth rules of conduct came to be worshiped after many long years. This is not right.

January 17, 1948

Many philosophies spring from the one source. Each has its purpose and fills the need of some individual. Each philosophy would not have evolved if it were not so.

The synthesis of them all is love of God, the Creator. Unseen, and beyond man's comprehension, He is the Father of all. A sincere desire to do His will is a requirement for attaining spirituality. All else follows. It is not only an intellectual pursuit, but one of the heart, also. Intellectual development is not to be belittled, however, since the brain is the instrument through which are gained experiences so necessary to spiritual growth.

May 3, 1949

An individual can train self by following rules set forth in various guides to living an enlarged life. The Bible is one such book. It is really an allegory of the development of an individual to just such living. It sets forth in allegorical form all an individual experiences while becoming a superman, as it were.

March 6, 1948

In the future, humanity will realize that there is something more to the Bible than stories. There are seven keys and it requires all seven to get a full understanding of it. The seven keys show the paths of man's attainment of cosmic consciousness. God helps humanity by endowing various individuals with special qualities so that they can help others and guide them in the right way.

June 10, 1948

The Patriarchs gained knowledge of God. Brains of men and their intellects were fashioned to comprehend the idea of God. Many writings speak of man's "fall" and development and give instructions for man to follow to again achieve blissful existence. The writings are either inspired or are products of some individual's intellect. Some have merit, and some rehash what has already been said very adequately by many individuals already. Man is allowed to develop at his own speed and no one's progress speeds up unless man himself wills it. The laws have been established and man lives accordingly. He must find himself; that is, his place in God's scheme.

Beliefs of an Esotericist   May 29, 1949

1. Belief in one God, who is the source of all being. God is not a person, but a Great Intelligence. That part of man which is eternal and everlasting is the part created in the image of God.

2. Belief in the goodness of everyone. It is not always apparent to others, because they have not recognized what the person is good for. Each

individual was created by God to do something in the world, and there is one thing that he can do better than anyone else in the world. Each person must discover and fulfill his mission in life.

3. Belief in respecting others' ownership of things. Stealing is the worst petty offense. God meant us all to have as much as we can use in fulfilling our missions in life. If we make the best possible use of what we have and use it to its full purpose we will not need for more. God knows better than we do what we need, and He provides without our asking.

4. Belief in one's immortal soul. There is a part of one which never sleeps, and which knows everything. Most of the time people are too taken up with outward stimuli to stop and listen to their souls speak. Under great stress, they shut out the noise of the world and pray fervently when all else fails. Invariably the soul gives the solution to any problem. The soul is very happy to do this.

5. Belief in keeping one day of the week holy. When God created the universe, He definitely set a pattern, which should be followed. Each person's cycle is different, and each was born at a different time, on a different day. Not all were born on the same day of the week; therefore, each one's Holy Day will be different. Whatever day it is, we should abstain from doing menial labor if we can help it, try to think only pure and holy thoughts, not say one unkind word or do anything mean. To discover one's seventh day of rest, one finds the day of one's birth first. That day is the first day, and the seventh day is the day of rest.

6. Belief in order. Cluttered surroundings make for a cluttered life. Effort must be made to keep all of one's effects in order. This exercise will lead to orderly thinking. Most untidiness comes from not finishing what was started. It is better to throw away or destroy unfinished business than to leave it lying around half finished. We must do the things which come to us to do if we wish to realize the full value of our lives.

7. Belief in living a strictly moral life. The body is the temple of the soul. As such it deserves the best that can be provided for it. Immorality leads to loss of respect for oneself and of oneself by others. A manner of

living never remains hidden for long. The eyes reveal the manner in which one conducts one's life.

8. Belief in adhering to principles of right in spite of opinions of others. If God reveals a great truth to one, which is yet not apparent to others, there is a trust to keep it alive. It is human nature to ridicule what it does not understand, and to destroy what is beautiful if it betters one's efforts. This is envy, because everyone thinks he knows everything and can do anything. And so he can, but not right away. It takes much study and practice. Unfortunately, most people are very lazy. A simple tiller of the soil will laugh at anyone spending many hours reading a book, painting a picture, or composing a piece of music.

9. Belief in accepting responsibility. If anything is owing to anybody, an individual should extend every effort to discharge the debt. If anything is promised, every means of honor should be made to fulfill the promise. If we find ourselves unable to fulfill the promise, we should pray and pray for God's help and try and try until we have done what we have promised. Nothing is impossible to God, and we probably made this promise, which we find we are unable to fulfill, to learn to recognize the power of God.

10. Belief in life. Only God has the power to give and to take life. Life is sacred and cannot be taken under any circumstances. This obviates capital punishment, wars (except in self-defense), and wanton killings of animals for sport; also, it eliminates vivisection.

Chapter Four

▼

Evolvement

December 20, 1942

God rotated the thirteen balls of fire with their constellations in such manner that this constellation should be the first to evolve spiritually.

March 2, 1948

Long ages ago, when the Earth was young, many strange animals roamed the Earth. Of these only one is left. That one is man. He has changed somewhat in appearance, but not too much. His seven vehicles are always constant in number. Only his densest, physical one has changed in appearance a little. Freshness of viewpoint leading to a different approach is about the only new feature added. He handles his problems more directly.

At first he lived wholly by what we now call intuition. Gradually, as he solidified, his physical brain took over the function of guiding him.

This was the beginning of all of man's troubles. The physical brain is too limited in ability to know everything.

March 12, 1949

In slowly advancing to perfect knowledge, the structure of a human's physical self changes. Perhaps the greatest change occurs in the individual's brain structure. Activity of certain cells develops centers which had never been used, or if they had been used, that use was slight. An individual's self centers upon activities of that immaterial self which is limitless, and many dimensional. When one considers that fourth and fifth dimensions are known to man, the mind staggers under contemplation of greater dimensions than these.

A human objective mind can know only those truths which it can grasp. Those truths that it cannot grasp, does not mean that they are nonexistent. An individual's objective mind has a very definite and tenacious life; and that life will scorn, ridicule and deny that which is not part of its experience.

Those in the human family who live by the objective mind alone whose minds are not developed enough to grasp truths concerning laws operating outside their sphere of mental and physical activity will, therefore, scorn, ridicule and deny that which is not obvious to their perception.

Many individuals are frightened when they awaken those centers in their physical bodies, the centers which are the receiving organs for the inner planes. They think they are losing their minds, and they deliberately shut off whatever impressions are received by the physical brain. This seeming dreamworld experience will increase more frequently on the physical plane, because humanity as a whole is evolving to the stage where fourth dimensional activity will be wholly natural. It will be helped at first, of course, by a means of communication of which radio and television is but a forerunner. An individual can communicate very easily with anyone thousands of miles away, and that instantaneously, by merely sitting in a comfortable chair, relaxing and projecting a conscious thought stream to another individual who receives it, if he, too, has those centers developed within himself which can receive that type of communication.

January 18, 1966

Actuality, translated into the reality of the human mind, appears dreamlike and flowing with continuous change and flux as the hallmark of everything in creation forever becoming. Nothing ever achieves a permanent status quo, with one exception.

Men have called the Unmoved Mover by many names. The names are legion. The names draw on ideas of the eternal and everlasting. All names agree on the One Alone from whom everything that ever was, everything that is, and everything that ever will be flows forth in an everlasting stream. The One remains ever hidden, and no human mind can ever know the quality or grasp the concept of the One's nature. A supreme miracle is that within each human consciousness exists the potential for knowledge of the law and order governing the universe. Analysis and synthesis exercise the mind considering the kaleidoscope presented by the limited vibratory range of the senses.

When the heart searches earnestly for answers to perplexities besetting the mind, the truth of the matter is shown in terms understandable to the level of the individual's consciousness. Consciousness reflects the One to the level of its evolvement and expansion.

August 20, 1960

Consider the evolvement of man since recorded history. The development did not come from without, but was unfolded from within. All evolvement goes on in this way, no matter which kingdom one wants to consider—mineral, vegetable, or animal. This ever-increasing complexity has a goal in view, nevertheless. Human consciousness cannot fathom the concept of the purpose and ultimate achievement of this evolvement going on in all kingdoms. We can say only that evolvement goes on until everything achieves perfection—so the matter stands and suffices, because man's ideas of perfection approximate the reality. Generally, the idea of perfection carries a connotation of cessation or a static stage when a certain level is arrived at, but that is not so, because nothing in the universe is static or ceases movement. All is life; all is motion.

It is for man a very difficult notion to accept the idea that all in creation is evolving and many more forms and combinations are coming into being in all kingdoms—mineral, vegetable, and animal, and also human. We owe our present state of being to how well we did our lessons in the school of life in previous life experiences.

January 18, 1960

The world "out there" is vastly different from the limited aspect communicated to us by our senses. Precognition, clairvoyance, clairaudience, and thought transmission, are some terms employed to designate means of contact with that greater world not apparent to ordinary sense perceptions. Experiences had throughout life can only be explained by these extrasensory perceptions. There are, of course, vast libraries on mysticism, occultism, religion, philosophy, metaphysics and the like extrasensory perception subjects which corroborate and explain that which is in that vast world beyond our ken.

Things become clearer and start making sense once the realization comes that a human being has other bodies besides the three-dimensional physical one which manifests in this three-dimensional plane of existence. Once a human being learns to use these other bodies of his by transferring his consciousness into them at will, he awakens to the realities of the world outside. The experiences of these less dense bodies are communicated to the physical objective brain once the link is vitalized and established between the other bodies of the human being.

All these remarks are as a touch of a fingertip to the vast ocean's surface.

Each individual will interpret the actualities of the outside world according to his own realizations, since his personality has its own aggregate of the stuff of the macrocosm. No two entities are alike, no matter on which plane of perception one contacts. Realizations of actualities will always differ. Some experiences will have no explanations for many, many years. At best, growth is a very slow process, taking up many, many lives. But, then, we have until all of eternity.

March 9, 1948

Many souls advance very slowly toward the Godhead because all their psychic centers take so long to open. Long familiarity with the subject does not necessarily mean that spirituality has been developed. Knowledge of it is not sufficient. Practice of correct living is the only way.

A stern unswerving faith in God and observance of laws governing right living is highly important in building one's soul body. Dedication of one's life to God is the simplest way. This does not entail a monastic experience. Life in the ordinary, work-a-day world can be carried on as usual.

September 21, 1960

Even the most material of men have realized, for ages past, that life and the universe have more to it than appears on the surface. It has puzzled mankind, and efforts are made to solve many riddles which present themselves; in fact, obtrude on consciousness. Those who devoted selves to an inner development to transcend the sum of evidence presented by the senses and an earnest desire to probe into the reality which lies beyond the field of contact of the senses have given to mankind guidelines for development. This development, searched for by many throughout humanity's history of being, has been discovered to consist of regular stages of inner unfoldment, which sharpens and enlarges the operation of the physical senses, then opens a duplicate set of senses which probe into the fields of higher vibrations. The study of unfoldment has revealed that man is a wonderful and unique creation. Men are just beginning to tap the surface of their own potential. In fact, there are only a very few who have reached any kind of real achievement in that type of self-realization. It all involves learning how to use the body and its mechanism correctly.

The greatest strides in this direction were achieved by the Orientals, but they lacked the drive and push to do something about it. That was one of the reasons the culture of the West was forced upon the mankind of the Orient. The outer physical self has to keep pace with the inner development. Constant attention to the inner functioning of the various parts has to be learned. But the hardest of all is to apply the various processes involved when one has learned them.

These processes have been the private property of various organizations throughout the world. In the West, the most notable one is the Roman Catholic Church. Within its archives are all the wonderful and mysterious results of various methods employed for many centuries by its Closed Orders in the business of developing and unfolding the inner faculties. This knowledge is considered dangerous to divulge to the unready. When one is ready, one presents oneself to a religious order and starts on the road of evolving methods suitable to oneself in becoming, in fact, a superman with tremendous powers. The danger lies in the use of these powers. Wrong use of them causes tremendous ill effects and harm. That is one of the many reasons why these things are not given forth to the laity. Indeed, most are not ready to receive the information or to apply it for the greatest good. Only those things for which all can benefit are given out. When they benefit only one to the detriment of others, then it is not good.

December 19, 1947

Lights shine with varying degrees of brilliance, depending upon the lamp. The same is true of people. Through some the spirit shines visibly, in some it is just a gleam, and some have not even been lighted. It is all a matter of vibration as far as the physical body is concerned.

January 26, 1960

Humanity has to make advances to catch up to where it should be in evolvement. It is very far behind. God may be like man in certain respects; but be assured, man is very un-Godlike. The Christ spirit can imbue a human with the power to make him Godlike.

January 31, 1962

Physically man is a water creature. Water is very important to man and the world. But man must have supremacy over that element. The element of water is also an enemy of man since it can and does absorb the physical part of him, but it can never have the soul part of him, because that is the fire part of him. However, the water element will always have power over the physical part of man until the fire part of him spiritualizes his physical body to the extent that he can walk on water like Jesus did. When his fire part is stronger than the water element in him, he will be able to command and subdue the monster of the water element, as Jesus did.

The power of water comes from Neptune. The power of Neptune is very great on Earth, because that is the element which is most plentiful. Fortunately, man can control it to some extent because of the salt in it. Salt is latent fire and man can control the violence of the oceans through his own fire working on the fire element of the salt in the waters of the oceans.

The reason for not eating meat has to do with the vibratory rate of the blood in animals, but this is as yet unknown to science and technology. Mankind does not have instruments capable of measuring the high vibratory rates of the energy emanated by blood cells in the animal kingdom. This will come in time. As a human evolves spiritually he can see and know this.

When one says that the human feeds on the animal kingdom it means that the spiritual man resides in an animal body and grows in consciousness through the uses and experiences gained by the body. This is a fine point, seldom realized.

April 5, 1955

In considering the human kingdom, we see a recapitulation of the lower kingdoms in man. Since man has an animal body, he draws sustenance from the lower levels. As he evolves into higher spheres of consciousness, his body becomes more spiritual, his vibratory rate increases, and he develops a distaste, even a repugnance for feeding on animal flesh.

January 5, 1948

Fundamentals of everything exist in the spiritual stage. All that is necessary is man's development to lift him sufficiently so that he may become *en rapport* with the world of ideas. This can only happen when man raises his vibrations through a knowledge of the laws which do so. The laws? The Sermon on the Mount contains about half of them. Master these and the others will be revealed.

December 19, 1947

A strict adherence to the teachings and instructions as set forth in the Sermon on the Mount will quicken the vibrations. The same goes for all inspired sets of rules concerning daily living. Man can also draw from the spirit many wonderful properties while raising the vibrations of his vehicle.

Communities and nations are the same as individuals. They are a body, too, through which the spirit shines. They are evolving, too, into perfect expressions of the spirit.

March 11, 1948

Control of the physical senses allows the spiritual to function more freely. In that way the mind is not cluttered constantly with what the body wants to do.

Pleasant experiences which contribute nothing to the soul's growth only sink the ego into contemplation of the terrestrial and do not act as a spur toward the spiritual. That is why man has all sorts of trials and tribulations so that he will not contemplate the physical plane solely.

Of the physical organs, the heart alone knows that the value of spiritual life transcends in excellency that of the physical. The heart transmits this message to the brain, which must give it voice. Since the heart is the abode of the Christ within, this is only natural.

January 23, 1960

When all ideas fail man, it is time to rely on imagination to fulfill functions which are attributes of the soul. Most of man's advances from arboreal existence were due to imagination. Nevertheless, the fact remains that the real progress was made because of soul progress with promptings which spoke to man inwardly. Jung has interesting things to say on this. He is both right and wrong; wrong in that he assumes that some individuals do not have this. Everyone has forces in this category which speak constantly, but man does not listen. That is the difference. Very few listen.

January 25, 1948

"Being" and "existence" are two different things. Being means a consciousness of life within, an awareness of a vital link with the Creator, an unmistakable knowledge of a Force. Of course, mere existence gives no such sensation to an individual. An individual, possessing free will, is at liberty to cultivate this channel in himself or not. The instructions are plainly set forth in many inspired works.

January 21, 1960

Although the vainglory's of the world enhance our senses, it is better to think of the eternal qualities of the soul first, and all else will be added unto it. Physical life entails certain responsibilities of soul to body; yet those are not as important as the body's responsibility to the soul. Therefore, instructions are necessary to allow unfoldment of soul qualities. It is important that one remembers first and foremost from where these instructions come. They must be heard with the inner ear. Some instructions are basic, but others are ramifications with individual applications. Each individual will have his own needs to be filled, according to his own unfoldment. All individuals are basically the same; we are all members of the human family. Yet, the fact remains that each is guided individually. No one is actually responsible to anyone else but to his own individual self. As members of social groups, of religious groups, of business groups, there are lesser responsibilities to maintain harmony within those groups—yet, the responsibility to oneself is the most important of all.

Duality December 29, 1947

Great Souls have either reached perfection by going through the laboratory known as the Earth, or proceeded from other regions unknown to us. Know this, only the Earth in the limitless galaxy teaches the way of the cross and the problem of duality. It is ever a source of interest to Great Intelligences who observe us carefully. Their sincere respect is accorded that trickle of souls who attain Mastership and rise out of the cycle of incarnations. A hard laboratory is the Earth, and those souls attaining Mastership earn every bit of respect. They shine with the burning light and vibrate with the high velocity of that Being which is higher than the archangels.

Yes, there is that heritage awaiting each individual. One only complicates the process when one refuses to listen to that voice within. Consequently, one does something else, which in pain refines the gross vehicle and lifts one's vibrations a shade higher. This may not be a pleasant process, but filled with pain and sorrow. Whatever happens, no matter how small or great, which affects an individual, the answer lies with the individual. A seeming injustice, a wrongful hurt, all are precipitated by the individual and work to raise the vibrations of his vehicle.

Man ever plods onward and upward, because he must. He is caught in the spiral out of which is no escape but by attaining Mastership. The works of organizations which aid in this process are of special interest to various Great Souls who are aiding in the evolution of the Earth and all upon it.

February 15, 1949

A man must contact fellow humans to gain knowledge, because that is the law of his being. Since physical man being nothing more nor less than a huge gathering together of cells, he is under the law of attraction and repulsion, because it is in his very being.

One is a common man and another is an aristocrat, because all must get experience in every phase of life. When universal observance of physical laws occurs, all humanity has learned the laws and they are no longer necessary. The laws, and the conditions making the laws, cease to exist.

January 6, 1948

Expansion and contraction, which are ever at work, are the two laws of duality. The idea is to gain enough insight into the object to realize at which stage it is, and use its potentialities to the full. This is where intuition is of invaluable aid. Intuition, properly developed, is infallible. Some Great Souls find this law of greatest interest because it is universal as well as one of the problems in duality on the planet Earth.

To work along with the development of an object or event is to master it; but to work against it is to suffer, because one cannot stop or alter the progress of the process in which the object or event exists. Find the phase, is the stern admonition.

Sometimes it is necessary to hold back a too violently spinning spiral so that it will be of some use to humanity, and to itself. This spiral of force can be a sphere such as the Earth, or even of such a fine substance as a human soul. Given time, it equalizes itself, finds its balance, and then it works to the good of all.

February 18, 1949

When the affairs of men reach a point where some help is needed to guide toward a good goal, the wisdom is given to the right ones. Also, the forces of darkness forever pit their forces to bring destruction and further departure from mirroring God. It is Nature's task to mirror the Creator. Some people can and do that very well, but others impose a will of their own and mirror only imperfection. Gladly would some mirror the Creator if they but knew how. That is the task of specially Chosen Ones—to lead the way to a self-realization and communion with God.

The mantle of earthly recognition means less then nothing. Only spiritual advancement leads to God.

December 20, 1947

Divine Wisdom has allowed Blessed Ones to work with various individuals and to help them establish love and harmony upon Earth. Dire results await those who have chosen the wrong path to prove their individuality. Given every opportunity to advance, they still prefer to go farther away from "home." The next lower sphere of manifestation is extremely painful to mankind. But mankind, having free will, may devolve if it wills to do so.

However, let us go on with looking at another facet of truth. It is only one vast truth, but various aspects of it are in manifestation at any time. Naturally, conditions upon the Earth allow only certain phases of the truth to manifest, which will teach the lessons of its sphere. This, of course, is the lesson of duality.

Repeatedly has this great truth been brought before humanity and the laws involved explained to various leaders so that they might set it in understandable form before humanity. Glancing at history, one sees that efforts of these Great Souls have led humanity steadily upward. It has been a slow and painful process. The human body, fine as it is, is still a very slowly vibrating agent and does not assimilate quickly or easily. Every truth upon Earth is a facet of the one great truth concerning duality. Every kingdom of manifestation illustrates this truth. When the creation of Earth was in process, some Great Souls became interested in observing the working of this law of duality and have even taken bodies to dwell among men. Being perfect in themselves, they have nevertheless gained additional color, which is vibration, through this experience.

Many God-sent individual souls came with special purpose and fulfilled this purpose. Men call these their Saviors.

There are many reasons why Great Souls incarnate in human bodies and do their work upon Earth. The Earth is a special sort of laboratory. It is of interest not only for its human population, but all other kingdoms of manifestation, as well. It is the only sphere upon which all conditions can manifest simultaneously. Each individual is in possession of a special virtue which he must set forth as an example not only in his group work, but outside in his family and in the endeavor at which he makes his living.

January 12, 1961

Consider the business of daily living further. When the individual attempts to have a life of some worth spiritually, all sorts of things conspire to prevent him from doing it. God lets people show all attributes of divinity if they only will to do so. Unfortunately man is so constituted that he can be coerced or put to sleep psychically to do others bidding. God lets men have freedom to grow spiritually. Men are in various stages of growth. They should be protected from evil influences, but there are not enough leaders who can do this. In fact, fortunately, as soon as man builds a mental body, he rises above the astral and cannot be reached by workers of the shadow.

March 21, 1949

People of the Earth work toward their own salvation, using the forces of truth, while a few use the forces of evil. The majority of humanity is unaware of being at the mercy of the forces of either kind. They follow their own instincts which arise from prompting of either good or evil.

Humanity must learn to discriminate and listen to only the good.

Sex December 19, 1947

A people's use of the sex power will decide their development. Since this planet is the school of duality, it is small wonder that this should be so. The correct use of this power is through marriage, of course. Divorce is unrecognized. A seemingly intolerable marriage between man and woman is a necessary process for each other's learning of various lessons. Divorce will not help, because when the problem comes again to the divorced individual it will be ten times worse, and he won't be able to do anything but bear it. The individual of a divorced couple who makes the move to go back to the other to give the marriage another chance is immediately released from this responsibility of facing the problem again.

Sex perversion and cohabiting with like is probably the worst sin, because it brings utter destruction.

December 15, 1947

The seething cauldron created upon Earth in these days is the work of the opposite element which strives to lower the Earth's vibrations to the next step below.

It is the work of the Brethren not to allow this. Since the world is the school of duality, the perfect union of the two is ultimately desired and not a further severance of the two opposing forces. Although they oppose, they are still working together to create a perfect whole. A further severance is disastrous because it leads to a still lower rate of vibration which is extremely painful to an individual composed of such elements as a human being. The sin of Sodom and Gomorrah is, therefore, to be strictly avoided, since it typifies this severance in daily living. It is sterile, lowers a human's vibrations, and leads to fire and destruction. It is a plague and a scourge of humanity. As soon as this custom becomes prevalent in a nation, that nation and all its people perish. Tell my people this.

December 19, 1947

Whoring is a waste of power. It causes deformity in the following incarnation, and a life of celibacy in some monastery or nunnery in the second next.

Onanism spills living seed, which Elementals use in building harmful thought forms.

The only way to use this power correctly is through marriage, and marriage alone. The moon regulation and observance of cycle will prevent a woman from conceiving if she cannot carry the burden. Flowing, cleansing agents are admissible. That is not an error.

Until man learns this, he will suffer.

February 15, 1960

The manifestation of homosexuality and lesbianism in society is laid at the door of parents most often. Usually this is true, and the unfortunate one who does not conform to the so-called norm is ostracized from society. He or she accepts this picture and crystallizes it. The problem is not solved by anyone. This Earth is a place of manifestation for a particular type of life. Life on Earth, embracing all kingdoms—mineral, vegetable, animal and human—express itself in terms of positive and negative, in terms of male and female, in terms of giver and receiver. Upon examining each kingdom of manifestation, one finds this basic law in operation. The law of the triangle—union of positive and negative, with the production (or potential of production) of a third manifestation—is the particular law of this plane of existence. In the human kingdom, when this law is not observed, there is an upset of the balance, and trouble results.

Eventually there comes the argument that there is a feminine polarity in a masculine body. Now, we are getting to the root of the problem. This is where parents have to be educated. Reincarnation being the fact that it is, souls change sexes of the incarnating ego, and though the soul is sexless, both aspects of manifestation are necessary to it. That is why it fell into matter and realized the pros and cons of life in matter. It is eating of the Tree of Knowledge.

Parents giving bodies to offspring should know the history of the incarnating ego to be able to help it. The incarnating ego must create a mental picture of the personality that it is to manifest. When the soul gives a male or female body to its personality for the first time after incarnating in the opposite sex, the transition is very sudden. But, the personality must live the life of the sex in which it is born. That is not the dictum of society. It is the dictum of the law of manifestation on the Earth plane; it is the dictum of the soul. The soul wants the experience of the sex that the body is expressing, and the body, being the tool of the soul, has to be obedient.

The question arises in the homosexual's mind: "How can I manifest the sex I am born into when all of my being cries for cohabiting with the same sex as myself?" The answer is simple. It is a matter of images. The soul presents the personality with an ideal image. It is the task of the personality to blend with and become that image—to love it to the extent that it is absorbed into one's being and one manifests it. The homosexual has this image, but instead of assimilating it into his own being and identifying with it, he holds it outside and worships it as it manifests in others of his own sex. He is failing his soul. He is failing in the task that his soul has presented to him as his life's work.

At first, it has to be a totally mental process to make that image one's own. There has to be a conscious acting out of a part, a conscious study in gestures, mannerisms, speech—in each aspect of expression and communication. It is not easy to act the part of a virile man when one is definitely effeminate. It has to become a constant practice to change the polarity for that particular incarnation. And it will take seven years of hard, concentrated, unremitting effort to effect this change. When it occurs there will be a demonstration of being a tower of strength. Self-discipline will be evident.

April 2, 1963

In many ways belief in God takes strange forms. Primitive man objectifies his need for added power and knowledge to cope with his environment. As man develops mentally and evolves inwardly, he turns more frequently into himself, somehow realizing that is where the source of all resides and is the door through which he must pass to realize the truth about all, if knowing the truth is possible for him.

Wine and money are man's greatest passions and the last to leave him. Despite popular opinion, sex is an appetite and a bodily requirement, like sleep. But man can sublimate it and use its creative power for other activities besides procreation. This is unique, because it is the only bodily appetite which can be sublimated.

May 5, 1955

Serpents are the electric and magnetic currents of the Earth. In symbolism they always represent the enchantment of earthly things and the false notion that immortality will come to man manifesting in his corporeal body with his physical senses. Most of humanity is focussed in its emotional consciousness, whose generating plant is centered in the solar plexus, which is fed by the creative energy of the physical body.

Man's ultimate destiny is spiritualization of self, and this is accomplished by the lifting of the body's creative energy to the heart, the throat, and, finally, to the head centers. Then, and only then, is man ready for conscious immortality. And the emphasis is on conscious.

There are many on Earth today who are unconscious of being very far along toward this goal. A criterion showing how far along an individual has progressed is his control of his emotional reactions. This does not mean that he is suppressing his emotions?not at all. His immediate reaction to an emotional situation is mental, as a matter of course. He does not become cold, unfeeling, or dispassionate. On the contrary, his understanding is such that his compassion and love, expressed in kindness and the will to help where help is needed, goes beyond that of ordinary human beings. But, at the same time, he does not get emotional about anything, and nothing upsets his equilibrium. If feelings and emotions are involved by any given situation, then one can be sure that he has not evolved enough to be a really constructive power.

Fate or Destiny February 24, 1960

Consider the fate of all people. It is as if they had a compulsion to do the things that they do. This compulsion, although it leads them to doing the things that they know they should not do, is nothing more than the balance adjusting itself and teaching them the lessons they should have. It is only after an individual starts having control over his own destiny that he can direct the things that happen to him, more or less. When people learn their lessons and the balance is adjusted, then one naturally has no need to repeat any experiences. That is the only way that man learns. Learning is a very slow process, but it is never ending, and humanity is gradually emerging into a semblance of what it is supposed to be—truly a natural, beautiful and noble creation of God. Most people are like animals, but that is natural, too, because man has an animal body to work with, and must make it divine.

February 22, 1960

Control of various bodies of manifestation—mental, emotional, and physical—depends very much on how one controls one's thoughts. There has to be the ability to switch one's thinking by sheer power of will. This is difficult, and more difficult than one realizes. Realization that one must control one's thinking is the first step in the control of the various bodies of manifestation. Recognition of this factor leads one to accept mastery of self and destiny. One's destiny is then shaped knowingly. Granted, it is difficult to fathom where this leads one, but in time, vision comes as well.

January 11, 1961

Now let us consider another aspect of ordinary daily living. When the time is ripe for an individual to face a certain experience in his own evolvement, he will be prepared inwardly to absorb the values and learn the necessary lesson so that he will evolve satisfactorily.

March 5, 1960

Everything which touches one's own life is of the utmost importance to everyone. Life is what one makes of it, and the connections one makes and the things one does are all important, no matter how trivial they may seem. Consequently, the fun of life is in the different possibilities that come up for inspection, deliberation and possible action. Perhaps the greatest of man's achievements came through in just such fashion.

February 19, 1949

The soul knows when an individual is ready to receive and work with a law of nature. Laws are not given until the individual is ready to work with them. Nothing in the universe stands still or is useless. Everything is in constant progress.

January 11, 1961

When mankind is ready for any development, as a whole, then the development comes. It is in the cosmic storehouse. Developments are already there. That is one of the basic justifications for belief in fate or destiny.

May 27, 1960

Time is simultaneous but the consciousness of people changes. People are living and existing in all ages simultaneously. And with each incarnation the consciousness switches from age to age and lives the life where it will learn its lessons best.

July 10, 1961

Man can even select the time segment in which to live, it seems. This is a great mystery. Nevertheless, it is true.

January 11, 1961

Long before any important event or happening is to occur, sensitive souls will have knowledge of it and will take action. In this way humanity, as a whole, has the choice of altering the personal connection with any event. If it is a particularly stringent thing, the individual can get out from under if he is determined enough to do so, and if he has the necessary strength.

January 13, 1961

Of great interest is the notion that things are predestined. Man can change the course of history. Knowledge can do this. The individual himself holds his own future in his own hands. The thought of greatness is in people's lives, too, if they choose so to make their lives.

The course of history is the same as the life of an individual, but in history there are many people involved, and they help one another in shaping events.

March 10, 1949

Worthy souls know inwardly all that is to be. They press forward, nevertheless, even though it results in pain. If some knew what was to be, they would try to change the course of destiny.

March 14, 1948

Individuals are allowed to work out their own destinies. There is wisdom in this, because if man were taken care of at every step, he would lose his initiative and never work himself up to where he belongs.

Long years have passed since man was guided at every step by angels. Frequently, one special individual comes on Earth, and he is constantly surrounded by angels, who shield him and guide him. The individual so protected never really lives wholly on the material plane, but accomplishes his mission and leaves incarnation. Several Great Souls sometimes come to Earth together to correct an existing situation. These work as a group and have great strength in that way.

February 4, 1960

When God created the world, there was a scheme put forth, a plan put into motion, and this is going on and on until all things complete their cycle and are withdrawn again.

Everything cherishes freedom and that is because each manifestation has a destiny to fulfill. Whatever interferes with that destiny is not good, and whatever furthers that destiny is good. People are not always aware of the fact that something is very good for them, although they may think it is not so.

Chapter Five

Education

January 20, 1948

Given a proper amount of training, any obedient vehicle can achieve earthly success, which in itself is nothing. The individual, however, learns a lot, which is most helpful to him.

All previous wrong training can be undone if the individual is obedient. God's ways are ever toward greater unfoldment of mind.

January 18, 1966

Formal schooling inundates the brain with others' findings and conclusions, which only give their grasp of actuality and what is reality to them. Education used as a springboard in expansion of consciousness serves its purpose for the mechanical process of getting knowledge regarding manifestation of creation apparent to the senses.

Since man is dual—material and immaterial—it is to his advantage to develop a link between the two—the positive and negative aspects of his being—and become a whole man.

The physical material part is the negative aspect. It is subject to, and at the mercy of, the laws governing cyclic changes—such as birth, growth, and decay—that manifested on our Earth and are perceived by our senses. The immaterial part is the positive aspect, with its attributes of eternal and everlasting being. The positive aspect is the immortal part of man.

April 1, 1949

Being is life, love and hope of achievement. The majority of humanity hopes to achieve something but are very vague as to the end and aim of all life everywhere.

Life follows a definite pattern, of course, according to laws of the universe. These laws are operating either forward or backward. The operations are not in a straight line, but in twirling triangular gyres.

Either one expands and evolves into another gyre of manifestation, or shrinks into a point and bursts forth into a lower gyre of manifestation. The shrinking is very painful.

August 20, 1960

We are aware of only the world which ordinarily obtrudes on our senses. We see only what our optical nerves carry to our brains. In like manner the same is true with all of our sense perceptions. There are some individuals who can see, hear, touch, smell, and taste on a greater scale than the majority. Unfortunately for them, the acceptance of their findings is fraught with difficulties because no one gives credence to experiences of someone else unless they can be duplicated by himself. We are really at a loss if we should communicate certain findings, provable to us; but others' senses are not as well or as finely developed as ours, thus we cannot have their corroboration. As it is, what we put forth should be regarded as a curiosity until time proves the statements correct. In short, all things, events, developments, are present here and now and can be seen, felt, touched, handled, but there is one difficulty: human senses are yet not as well developed as they can be to perceive everything.

July 12, 1966

A necessary corollary to communicating intelligence is a personal intimate knowledge of the subject. And when the field of knowledge encompasses realms of perception closed to the ordinary physical senses, the immediate task is employment of simile, analogy and correspondence comprehensible to individuals oriented solely to the physical sense perceptions of the five senses. Animal man is so constituted electromagnetically that he can extend the range of his sense perceptions through diligent continuous effort of his mental power. Through employment of reason and extended application of reasoning powers to considering the abstract world of ideas having no physical manifestation, man is pushing and/or being pushed into realizing his potential of becoming a true human being.

Immediately comes the query on how to differentiate animal man from a true human being. The difference is in Mastery, which always is accompanied by power. Mastery comes with knowledge, but knowledge is only a gateway for a breakthrough into a world of reality which men call wisdom. In the history of man's manifestation as a reasoning being, very few have attained this stage. Of these few, thousands of tomes exist as testimony and as guides for the pitiful few strong enough to storm these worlds of reality transcending the objective world as known by animal man. How does one communicate intelligence for which there are no words to convey meaning to the deaf and blind? How to unstop the ears and tear off the blinds, thereby extending their range of perception? Fortunately, man's inherent dissatisfaction with things as they are, drives him further and further into abstract thought activity. The experiences of visionaries are finding corroboration here and there.

Sooner or later an isolated individual gathers up enough courage to face the terror of himself and what sort of animal he really is. He soon discovers his patina of civilization and culture is pitifully thin. It is one thing to be an animate compendium of other people's knowledge and findings, but quite another to really know that which is beyond the frontiers achieved by man before. Of necessity, it must be so, otherwise there would be no Newton, Einstein, Wagner, Edison, and others of that ilk.

Perception comes from within one's being, depending upon reaction to varying qualities of stimuli. Should the receiving apparatus of the physical self be insensate to particular rates of vibration, no amount of exposition will communicate the effect of stimuli. That field of knowledge will forever remain a closed book to the insensate one.

March 17, 1960

Level of intelligence is not an untruth. It is a very true thing. Long years of experience will train the mind along certain lines, but that is not the same thing. Level of intelligence is an attribute of the soul. It is something that the incarnating principle brings with it when it comes to inhabit a newly born body.

April 19, 1948

Only those of superior intelligence know and see ahead the conclusions to a set of actions. This comprises omniscience. There is nothing wonderful or amazing about it. It is a perfectly normal function, once the inductive and deductive powers have been developed.

January 28, 1960

What of development? That is the prime objective of humanity. Whatever the soul's properties, it still needs to grow, get greater light, or enlargement. Being a ball, shining white, and covered with eyes, it still needs evolvement. The only way in which it can grow and evolve is through experiences of the human body as it goes through the business of daily living. That is the chore of the body. One asks—what is the use of it all? Evolvement is a law of nature—like growth, transformation, flowering, etc. It is the way things are and there is nothing we can do about it.

March 17, 1960

Yes, this applies to animals, too. When an animal is close to individualization, its soul does not go into the common reservoir of its particular kingdom, as it were. It waits for another body; and, aided by the master spirit of its kingdom, it is reborn to be with a more intelligent family so that its progress will not be impeded.

April 5, 1955

The spiritual universe, of which the material is the image, is a world of forces—energies which in crystallization assume the varied material appearances. Bringing the consciousness to bear upon and contemplate this manifestation of concertized energy shows varying frequencies of activity, which man's consciousness calls vibrations.

Consciousness and its evolvement are the prime factors deciding the progress of humanity.

November 3, 1954

God brought humanity out of further involution by His Love, but man recognizes it not until he keeps God's Commandments and evolves to the stage where he becomes actively conscious of his own divinity and knows there is God. God bestows upon man a faculty of knowledge and reason by which man can evolve into a superhuman entity, but the task lies wholly within himself.

December 29, 1947

Knowledge in itself is of little value. It is true that it raises one's vibrations, expands the horizon, and enlarges the understanding. It is the application of knowledge which is of utmost importance. This is what makes for a still greater capacity for acquiring it.

More people would acquire this wisdom of the universe if they heeded the prompting within. These promptings may suggest following a line of action that is entirely foreign to the individual's way of life. He may even reject it as a temptation and by that cut off the flow at its source. How can one judge a temptation? By asking if it hurts anyone, or if there is a possibility of it hurting anyone. Then a perusal of the Sermon on the Mount in relation to this line of action should determine whether any of the laws are being broken. If there is no transgression, follow these promptings from within, and a new life will open.

The human body is a wonderful mechanism. It can be a perfect servant for the soul, or it can be a total obstruction to the soul's will to work. And it is right that this should be so. As the soul is ready to work, so is a finer vehicle provided to serve its purpose.

Sometimes many decades are necessary to bring a person's idea to fruition, and at other times it is only a matter of moments. Wherein lies the answer? The answer lies in the body's ability to be a fit vehicle. The greatest single action is power of thought and intentness of mental imaging. Together with this power of thought, the beat of love from the heart makes for an uplift which lifts the individual into the category of being a real human.

August 25, 1964

Actually, one can learn a tiny bit at a time. What is called "learning" is bringing up to the surface what one had learned in many, many lives—hundreds and thousands of them. That is why children get so self-assured in a stage they go through—some in high school and some in college, when they feel they know everything. And that is the point at which they catch up with what they have known all during their past lives. It is after this stage has been reached, and they have settled down somewhat, that they start applying the knowledge they have gathered in the past. As they apply what they already know they discover new things, and thus learn more.

January 17, 1948

Strength of will and purpose is a direct product of the intellect. This attribute is a much needed ingredient in the education and development of the immortal soul. Learning is a necessary adjunct but not the final accomplishment.

Naturally, our learning will be of the sort to conform to our vibrations. A healer will not profit greatly by studying jurisprudence. He will gain some knowledge, of course, but will not reach the peak of thorough knowledge and perfection in his art because his vibrations are not attuned to it. A child should, therefore, be allowed to develop and reveal his potential before a particular profession is inflicted upon him simply because his physical forebears followed it. In that way, his intellect will flower unhampered and his practice of his profession will be a definite blessing and contribution to struggling humanity.

The sum of this lesson is to allot a place to development and growth of the intellect. Care should be taken that it does not shut out the voice of the soul, but that it should become a fit and noble instrument of the soul.

January 9, 1961

Consider life in general for a moment. The most fruitful experience obtainable in life is the one from which man, or woman for that matter, makes his or her living. Therein will be found the field of experience, which is needed by the soul for its own evolvement. The chosen profession does not just happen, but it has to be truly the chosen profession of the soul.

Mission in Life March 28, 1960

God prepares various individuals and gives them missions to accomplish. All people have a mission. That is why they feel important. Necessarily each individual is an egotist, and with reason. Each has an appointed task. This task, he or she can do better then anyone else. It is the frustration of this purpose in each one's life which leads to ills of mankind. Many factors interfere with people's lives, not the least of which are parents.

September 3, 1964

Every human being born has a mission to fulfill. There is not one superfluous person in the world. The number of souls in incarnation and out of incarnation is a fixed number.

In view of this, every child has a mission. When parents, through ignorance, do not help their offspring fulfill the mission, they themselves draw an adverse consequence. The pity of it is that at some period in every child's life, he or she knows what its mission is and what it wants most to do in life. Most often, parents refuse to accept the child's choice.

In the modern world, the Jews are probably the wisest people in this regard and do whatever they can for their children to accomplish their mission. The Orthodox ones are much wiser in this regard than the Reformed.

April 20, 1960

God wants a new resurgence of faith and works to give humanity a further push forward. The time has come for humanity to realize that there is a reason for each person's birth on Earth. Every human being has a mission to do which will benefit not only him but all of humanity as well. This mission is known to the soul, and it must communicate the knowledge to the physical intelligence. The method was clearly described by Jesus when he urged the stilling of one's inner turbulence, and going into the silence and peace within to contact the knowledge of the soul.

February 8, 1948

Given a specific problem to solve, the average man brings his objective mind to bear upon it and works until his objective mind becomes so tired and weary that it subsides and the inner mind comes through the barrier to give the answer. Then the individual congratulates himself on his ability and boasts of his inspirational powers.

If that individual had learned to contact his inner consciousness at will, he would have saved himself a lot of work in the first place.

Intuition is a perfectly normal function of man.

January 27, 1948

Individuals hearkening to the call of the flesh exclusively can have no progress in intuition, wisdom, or peace of mind. Theirs is a torturous existence. They are extremely unhappy. Why? They think of nothing else but self. It is only when an individual stops thinking of self and starts to think of doing some good to the world that the person begins to know happiness.

Meditation January 8, 1948

Find some means to communicate with your own soul. That is the rule which men should try to follow. Once in touch with his own soul, man has to live a noble life.

How to reach one's soul? There is nothing easier and nothing harder. All one needs to do is be absolutely still, and the soul will speak. Sit, or stand at ease, and focus the thoughts on one subject. Think only of it. As the physical brain activity ceases creating its own random images, the soul comes through and speaks. To some the soul will communicate in music, or in song, and to others as in pictures. Whichever form of communication the soul chooses is the form best suited to the individual. The knowledge which is imparted from the soul is from God. When man learns to do this he will have attained his true mission on Earth.

March 4, 1949

A soul name is a rate of vibration. As no two souls are alike, no two names are alike. The rate of vibration is music, too. So a soul name is a musical phrase or chord. It is also a color, a color being a rate of vibration. The predominating note or color is that of the ray from which an individual is an emanation.

Sometimes soul names have no corresponding sound upon the physical plane. We can only approximate it. The soul name is something an individual, when he discovers his own, has no doubt about. He knows. It is something no one communicates to him. He awakens to it himself, because his soul name is really made by himself. His soul name is the sum of all his experiences in all his incarnations.

February 10, 1960

Meditation proves fruitless if there is no plan behind it. That is why it has to be done under guidance and with order. One takes color and form into consideration, also sound. Where the soul has already evolved toward perfection, even a little bit, the inner intelligence can sometimes serve as a guide. The Masters are ever on the lookout for evolved souls, and there is no chance of an evolved soul to go unnoticed. Granted, there are many holy people in the world and they seem to be alone, but that is not true. They are under constant guidance and surveillance. They keep themselves in tune with the cosmic and are guided thereby. Thus, group work is essential for the masses. Single effort has to be under guidance.

January 10, 1948

Give meditation full allocation of time each day. Be systematic. Choose the same period of the day to meditate. This systematic observance will establish a rhythmic swing, or spiral which will aid greatly in development. And that is the prime reason for establishment of group meetings at specified times. Regular attendance will put the individual inside the rhythmic undulation and one's benefits will be more than one can realize.

The individual can establish an own rhythm between the terrestrial and the cosmic, but it must be at the same time each day. The preference is very late at night or early in the morning, because there is less disturbance of the atmosphere from thought waves of people, most of whom are asleep at this time.

February 19, 1948

To rise above the effects of the Earth's vibrations it is necessary to learn to retire within, and this elevates the consciousness. Men must learn this because it is part of their training in their heritage.

From the beginning, the Earth has been an object of special solicitousness by the Great Ones. The affairs of men have been carefully watched.

July 31, 1960

When the Lord God decided to influence mankind toward the righteous path after it had transgressed, He sent an emissary to appear in a vision to the most advanced of the people, who, in turn, communicated it to the people. Thus, it was in early Bible days. Today more and more souls reach up to cosmic consciousness and attune themselves to the plane of wisdom.

There is one sure method of attuning, and that is daily periods of meditation. Meditation is the only answer; and the wisdom, nay, the pure necessity of meditation makes it advisable to pursued it without delay. Indeed, at least five minutes a day must be devoted to the task of meditation. Some thought must be selected and some symbol, then meditation done on them. This will open floodgates of veritable treasures, which will solve not only one's problems but can be used to solve problems of others when they need help.

January 18, 1966

It behooves each individual to note down scrupulously each dream occurring, and gradually get to know his symbology, which is uniquely his own and like no other. In this way, the individual will discover his own law of being.

April 5, 1960

Elevation of thoughts leads to contact with a veritable storehouse of wisdom. Perhaps the practice will become a natural function of all, in time. To know when to do the right thing, when to make the right choice, indeed, to know what the right choice is, at all, is the epitome of wisdom. So few know this instinctively and so few have the faculty of prevision to see the outcome of any action. Action is the outcome of necessity, of need for fulfillment of some prevailing condition. This is the reason that so few know exactly which way to turn and what action to follow.

March 10, 1960

Great thoughts are the results of concentrated single-pointedness on some given subject. Through much effort, attention deepens into meditation, and through further effort, it deepens into contemplation. Then all facets of a given subject (or aspect thereof) are explored by one's being, and the result may bring forth an entirely new idea, or an original presentation of a very old idea which has been abstrusely presented before. Thinking is not difficult; but thinking for results require effort, which spells work—sometimes very hard work. That may be the reason school children, in the majority, detest school, because it forces them to think along a particular line, and that is work. Adults feel the same way, too.

January 24, 1948

The round of human activity tends to sweep one on to spirituality. Everywhere people are beginning to realize that there is something beyond the visible manifestation.

Greatness of character denotes greatness of soul or greatness of the force working through that particular human. Men can make themselves great by following the dictates of their souls. From that source they automatically rise to greatness. The greatest force in the universe is God; therefore, he who would be great should establish contact with God, and greatness is his automatically.

Framing of a resolution is the first step. Then devote the same hour every day to meditation on the inward self. One should have a sincere desire to hear the Voice of God. This will bear fruit more quickly and easily than one realizes.

January 12, 1948

Greatness of soul pertains to high rate of vibration. In man it should apply to great intellect and learning.

May 5, 1949

What makes man a great soul is knowledge, which imparts brightness and brilliancy to the vibration of his soul being. Knowledge on this plane comes by pain and tribulation for most people.

January 12, 1948

Formlessness of thought characterizes an undeveloped intellect. Only through strict discipline of the physical brain can real thinking be taught, and that is the value of meditation.

Truth May 3, 1949

Truth is an irrevocable fact, an actuality which exists regardless of man's cognizance of it. The highest truths have to be sensed and felt, since they may not necessarily belong to the objective plane of manifestation. Naturally the higher aspects of all three-dimensional manifestation can be known, since they are but a higher vibration of the objective manifestation.

December 15, 1947

A truth is that which perfectly reveals a law in operation from everlasting being, and to which everything that was, is and ever shall be, is subject. A knowledge and understanding of a truth will raise a person's vibration considerably. An application of the truth in one's life raises these vibrations tenfold and leads to Mastership. Ultimately, only one great truth exists, and knowledge of it leads to union with God. This truth has many rays which touch and illumine every individual. As one tiny ray enters the heart of an individual, it enlarges the person's understanding so that the ever-widening ray will find lodgment therein—and on until the one vast truth is absorbed by the perfect soul. One of these perfect souls is Jesus. As example of His perfect living can lead many, many souls to absorb the one great truth.

January 23, 1960

Men grope for truth on all subjects, but there is no complete truth on anything, only relative truth. All things possess a true and false aspect, but even truth as we know it has some untruth in it. It has to, because otherwise it could not exist in this negative world of manifestation. To manifest, it must have negativity. If it had no negativity at all, it would be unmanifest. In fact, we would not be aware of it at all physically.

December 14, 1947

When two souls gather the forces of a truth beyond ordinary man's comprehension, all capacities of mankind to assimilate the knowledge of this truth are automatically created in man. This process is well illustrated by the pebble being cast into a body of water which will be disturbed down to the last particle.

Why two souls? The Earth carries the lesson of duality. When a particular vibration containing a truth is played upon the Earth from any of the four corners of creation, there is always someone ready to gain possession of it, enough to translate it into speech. Now, why two? One of these will illustrate the positive effect and the other one the negative. The rest of mankind is awakened by the play of the vibrations upon the Earth, and their faculties are opened enough to recognize the truth when it is eventually presented in either or both aspects.

March 3, 1945

A man's soul is his own private business, and he builds barriers against prying.

All philosophies are true and all are false, because every one of them presents facets, but not the whole truth. The student accepts or rejects them, according to his own understanding. He may even present quite another facet arrived at through sheer inspiration or methodical deduction. This facet, if true, will stand the test of time.

Selection and rejection of ideas are as natural to man as breathing. There are no two alike in creation, and there are no two parallel minds. Disciples question their Masters and differ in points of view, which is wholly natural.

To possess all knowledge is to possess all power. Mankind is not developed enough to know everything about everything. Knowledge in itself is a cycle within a spiral gyration, and each cycle takes in some more territory in the field of knowledge as it strives toward all knowledge.

No civilization is totally lost. Things worthy of survival, because they have an element of truth in them, are necessary to the knowledge of the next cycle, and thus live on. There is no sharp line of demarcation between civilizations as they blend one into another. "Wheels within wheels" is an idea that applies to civilizations, nations, individuals, animals, plants, and even the tiniest atom.

March 5, 1949

The reason for old philosophies coming to the fore is that some ancient Atlanteans with the old blood type of structure have been reborn and they require old methods of attaining illumination.

Deep meditation will show that their blood is different and they can take the old initiation, while some cannot because the blood is constituted differently.

Yes, man, know thyself before you experiment with your vehicles. Do not destroy your vehicles, because they serve you.

All those who dwell in darkness scorn the light. They think theirs is the normal state of being. And those who dwell in the light must pity and give help, if possible, to aid the ones in darkness to find comfort in the light. What men need are a guide and teacher. Should he observe accurately, he would not require a mentor, but he does not interpret correctly what he sees, so he requires an interpreter—at least at first.

Humanity needs a perpetual show of cause and effect. People are so prone to forget causes when they see only the effects. So few can reach back and deduce the cause to create a particular effect.

February 11, 1949

God-inspired ideas have a permanency, which ordinary thoughts do not have. Ideas which are truth are everlasting. Man's idle thoughts or verisimilitude's may have a life cycle, depending upon how much of truth they contain, and then they vanish when their usefulness is over. Thus, it is with everything in creation. That which is truth will alone prevail everlastingly. That is why it is vitally important for men to so develop their soul powers that only truth will be reflected. This truth will be the saving, the way to everlasting life.

Nature and form are evanescent, a means to an end. By extracting from them all truth as expressed, man uses both as his tools in his striving toward God. Time will obliterate both, because both are subject to time. Only that which is everlasting and permanent is not subject to time.

September 16, 1959

Ideas collide when they are originated by separate individuals. The truth of the matter is that each individual prefers to preserve his supremacy. All ideas have a common origin, but each individual thinks his idea is better. There is no such thing as a second best idea. It is either tops or not tops at all. Human beings, as they are constituted, must perforce share their ideas, because an idea pushes itself out to demonstration and will show whether it is good or not. The criterion is, of course, that the demonstration must benefit and bless all who become exposed to it. If the result is violence, bloodshed, or a deprivation of basic needs, then it is not good.

December 30, 1947

Evolving vehicles spare not themselves nor others around them. Everyone is for himself. The rush and process are done with such determination that it brooks no interference. And that explains the seeming cruelty of nature and of animal man. It is only the ever forward, relentless drive of evolution.

Bring forth a new idea and it has to be assimilated. Everyone rushes to experience it. The hunger for experience is truly phenomenal. It is so contagious that even truly Great Souls incarnate to gain experience.

Follow any idea to it's very end and you will have gained a marvelous experience. Its effect has imprinted itself upon you forever and has become a permanent part of your being. Nothing can destroy or take any part of it away. That explains the prevalence of selfishness and greed. It is the opposite side of the natural hunger for experience. Where one ennobles, the other demeans and causes vast suffering. And suffering is an experience which contributes to growth.

Know all this for what it means.

January 16, 1948

Well-being in this world depends upon one's balance achieved in both worlds. Great Souls always work through individuals who have achieved that balance, because it does not interrupt the flow of ideas.

Many problems of life are created by the individual, and it is right that this should be so. How else will the individual experience the various phases of life, which are his instructions? Let a new idea manifest, and every one rushes to have the effect of experiencing it.

Follow ideas to their source to detect their origin—to either the positive or negative aspect of the one Great Source.

August 12, 1961

There are a few misconceptions needing straightening out. In the world there are so many half-truths, untruths, and downright deliberate lies that it is a wonder how man arrives at half the things he does, although he does not know many things. Life is one long struggle for him. He can or cannot fathom some truths. Some truths require another kind of knowledge which man does not possess yet. Time will come when he will. Right now his senses are not refined enough to know the truth of some things which cannot be explained in terms of the physical. In fact, they do not manifest in the physical at all. They influence the physical, and that is something which men must learn to expand their knowledge.

Inspiration February 9, 1949

A very few men and women can probably tell you what their highest ideals consist of and what their aspirations are. But the majority do not think beyond their immediate wants or aspirations. Inspiration may be spontaneous at times, but in most of people it is a slow laborious process, arrived at only after long meditation and cogitation upon any given subject. So it is with all great problems of life. Nothing is solved overnight. It takes a careful pinning together of facts and ideas, then working them out to a logical conclusion. Long hours of hard mental labor goes into the fashioning of a piece of work which is usable. Imaging in the mind is perhaps the most important function of the human mind.

July 6, 1960

Where does one find inspiration? One finds it within, and only within one's own being. To deny inspiration's manifestation is a self-deception or plain laziness. A person does a great deal of disservice to himself when he does not pay attention to inspiration. To act upon inspiration is to be truly under guidance of one's soul, which is an attribute of divinity.

The soul presents ideas, and the mind interprets them objectively so that the individual will understand what the soul is presenting for meditation and to add to one's store of knowledge, to be remembered always.

January 6, 1948

Full realization comes when all do their work properly. By full realization is meant a manifestation or demonstration. First, the impulse is sent forth from the spiritual plane. Human individuals sufficiently developed get the idea and realize its details. Plans are made and the idea is given form. It becomes an object. Everything that has ever found expression on Earth came forth thus.

February 14, 1949

Only greatness of spirit gives complete understanding. If the mind is great, the individual will understand. When the soul contacts the brain center, there is great rejoicing in the universe. Many do so unconsciously. Also, inspiration and illumination are nothing else but the breaking through of divine knowledge contained in the soul, to the conscious mind. Of such stuff are all great enduring things made.

Many think that a clever individual reasoned out great truths. In every instance the individual contacted the divine principle within himself and learned the truth of the matter under consideration. Since truth is enduring and bodies are perishable, people have to contact their overshadowing principle, the principle which is permanent, to learn the truth. Frequently many poets and great writers have said this, but in such obscure terms as to be meaningless except to the initiated. In times past, this caution was necessary, but humanity is evolving with extreme rapidity and there are thousands of unconscious Initiates in the world today, so that facts like these can be disseminated without fear of misuse.

January 20, 1948

Inspiration and love are identical. It may not seem so, at first glance, but reflection will show that this is so. It is true that different objects inspire that emotion, and it seems to take two sets of entirely dissimilar stimuli to create either effect; but in the final analysis, inspiration and love are the same thing.

December 17, 1947

England gave a few interpreters of truth to the world. Also, France and Germany. These Western nations gave not as many as the Eastern, but they are more known, and their names are household words.

Now America's turn has come. More interpreters of God's word are needed. This necessitates a selfless dedication and a thorough cleansing of the body, so that the stream can flow uninterrupted.

Love of fellow man is the first requisite. Tolerance and patience are needed, too. Many virtues and high learning are not requisites to become a fit vehicle. A strict observance of the Golden Rule is about all that is required.

Jesus chose His followers from among the simple folk. Andrew had learning, also Mark, but the others had not enough to warrant their being called scholars, yet their work has endured many centuries. No—great learning can sometimes be a hindrance. What is a learned man but a walking compendium of other men's ideas? If he received an original thought, he would probably reject it simply because no one else had said it. An unlearned man will take it, marvel at it, accept it, publish it, and then be quoted by learned parrots for centuries. This admonition is a necessary part of all teachings, to point out that no man or woman should decry his or her lack of education. Worldly education, like fine raiment, is merely a covering up of essentials. Only love can raise or quicken the inner vibrations so that the stream of inspiration will flow through it unimpeded. And this stream will carry all the wisdom there is.

July 17, 1948

Love breaks down the hardened astral shell of the individual and enables him to express the ideal man which he must first imitate, then become. Love is the greatest emotion of which man is capable. Physical love is only a poor reflection, but the first one which a person can use to lead him to Divine Love.

February 12, 1948

Love reigns in humanity in its lower aspect closely allied with animal passion. This love is slowly purified by the individual when he transmutes it into Divine Love.

April 28, 1961

Love is the greatest single factor in God's creation, and it holds the universe in place.

The Classics February 26, 1949

Great literature, music, drama, dance, in fact all exponents of the artistic expression have a place in humanity's progress. Only those works which are of great value are works of genius and will be permanent inasmuch as they can be permanent in the three-dimensional world where nothing is permanent.

December 17, 1947

Form and substance are needed to manifest truth. Do not scorn your body. It is a manifestation of truth. So are all beautiful things. We instinctively know what is beautiful, and the knowledge and appreciation of it will raise the inner vibrations.

Incidentally, that is the test of all enduring works. If they raise the inner vibrations to a better knowledge of God they are immortal, because they manifest a law. It does not mean that a statue, painting, book or piece of music will last through eternity. It means that these outward forms will endure as long as man needs this particular illustration of a truth. Yes, there are objects that have endured thousands of years.

March 29, 1948

In accordance with all great works of art, literature must raise the soul's vibrations if it is to endure. Otherwise, it will be forgotten and discarded soon after publication.

Long ages pass, still some works persist, seemingly imperishable. In each generation they do their work in awakening souls. Of such stuff are the Iliad and the Odyssey. We call these works classics.

The same applies to music, painting, sculpture.

Incidentally, the Iliad and Odyssey were originally songs.

June 2, 1957

Objects, dwellings, buildings, even surroundings, are all impregnated with vibrations. A beautiful thing can have vibrations that are inharmonious, depending on its usage. Until one has developed the "third eye," one cannot say positively that some things are good, and some are bad.

March 20, 1960

The astral body's concretization has been broken down—which is the purpose of percussion music. The purpose of beat music has been to do this. Painting: cubism and abstracts are expressions of angry people.

When peace is made with self in relation to the world, then the painter is happily painting happy expressions of self. One can only express what one feels and knows. There is a vast discontent in the world. This is the secret of man's progress, incidentally, this discontent.

November 11, 1954

Greatness in a human depends on how well an individual is attuned with the eternal principle within. The more constant and perfect the channel, the greater the individual will be. Greatness in art expression is entirely dependent on this rapport, but it is not limited to the field of art expression. It may be any field of endeavor. Also, the Christ within must be well reflected in order for one to generate the high frequency power necessary to express adequately. Greatness naturally follows. It cannot help but be. And that is the goal of every soul in or out of incarnation.

December 28, 1947

Great works are always given forth when the people are ready to assimilate them. First, the stream of humanity is purified by one means or another. Wars, pestilence, and catastrophes take their toll, and those souls wait till they can incarnate in better surroundings among better people. It is not always sinful people who are taken out of incarnation in catastrophes, epidemics, and the like. The good people are given new bodies almost immediately. This explains the rising birth rate after every sweeping catastrophe. Man must always go forward whether he likes it or not, because that is the scheme of things. Greatness is thrust upon him. He must learn to wrap that mantle around him and live up to it—in humility.

September 18, 1948

Divine messengers are sent to humanity in various forms. It is not only in the flesh that God's emissaries manifest. They come in spirit, as well. Humanity is aware of them as great reforms, inspirational literature, art or music, and ideas of vast concept affecting nations or the whole world.

There is good reason for spiritual manifestation as explained above. If an idea bursts forth from several minds at once, the chance of it sweeping over a large portion of humanity is greater than if it were the concept of only one mind.

When a nation follows an idea, though it is erroneous, it is only because as a nation it needs to be taught the lessons attached to that idea.

Thought Power May 5, 1955

Weather is caused by the collective thoughts of man. The invisible world is peopled by Elementals which should be ruled by man. But in his fallen state, man can hardly rule himself without even thinking of the elemental world. The vibrations man sets up stimulates the elemental world in one way or another. The effects cause all sorts of things from hurricanes and tornadoes to droughts and tidal waves. Man is a mighty being with an awesome and frightening power.

May 1, 1960

Man is seen as an ordinary sleeping and mesmerized creature. Sleep is induced by the obedience under which the individual is born. Before any individual can make any kind of progress, he must be awakened. Souls have to withstand all kinds of shock to be awake. There are rhyme and reason to being asleep. Otherwise, people would go absolutely mad to see the chaotic state in which humanity exists. Although there is strict discipline exerted by the various hierarchies, the awful truth exists that humanity is misusing its powers frighteningly. All the ills on Earth are caused by mankind. That is true. All the ills of the Earth, such as great storms and catastrophes, even the climate, are caused by man. People seldom, if ever, intentionally do good. There is always even the tiniest hint of self-interest.

May 5, 1955

There is a terrific amount of sin accumulated on the Atlantic coastline, and also on the Pacific one—but, the Atlantic has more, as a whole. On the Pacific, San Francisco, Sitka, and Los Angeles, in that order, have accumulated sin over the longest spans of time. Sin hangs like a dark cloud over each locality. When the negative destructive forces overbalance the positive preserving ones, catastrophe occurs. The nature of the catastrophe is determined by the type of destructive force accumulated. When and where destruction will occur is determined when the balance of evil outweighs the good.

For instance, there is a gigantic black claw-like hand stretched out over New York City. It is held at bay by the constructive action of people. The daily Masses said by the Catholic churches build up protection. The daily Bible lessons recited by the Christian Scientists and similar organizations contribute to the protection of the city. A convention of the Seventh Day Adventists can clip the claws of that hand. It takes many months of evil, constantly being emanated, to grow new claws.

Who can foretell when the power of that hand grows to such strength that it will descend and destroy the city? It all depends on the collective thoughts and actions of the people there. The thoughts and actions of the ones dedicated to Christ's service may burn up the hand completely.

February 25, 1960

Kind thoughts have a reward, since they create a vibration in one's aura which has great strength and does not allow negativity to enter the aura. Kind thoughts do not take an especially forceful method, because the fact of their peace and harmony give them strength. On the other hand, thoughts that need vehemence take much effort, like thoughts of anger, of envy, of greed—these thoughts really take up much energy. The odd part about it is that they create a weakness in the aura—even holes, they create—through which negativity can enter. That is why there has been all this talk on positive thinking. This positive thinking is what makes things happen which are beneficial to one's well-being, to one's health and prosperity.

February 4, 1948

Vibrations of a single mind can reach thousands upon thousands of miles. Another thing, similar ideas attract each other, and two people having the same idea can have their thoughts commingle, which results in their meeting one another on mental planes, most often. Therefore, people should be careful how they think. Thoughts are living things.

Chapter Six

Teachers

February 15, 1960

Those teaching today, and in previous years down through history, are for the most part, inadequate. Teaching is more of an art than a profession. In fact, it is a most noble calling. The ability to create a clear mental image is one thing, but to evoke that same image with the same clarity in another mind is quite another. This involves communication; and to really teach, it is of the most vital importance to be able to communicate.

It is not enough to create the mental image in the mind of another. The learner must then be able to communicate it back. This aspect of teaching is sadly neglected. Calling upon pupils to recite or to give them tests, or to give them examinations is still not filling the need. Each lesson is not learned thoroughly enough when the teachers go on to the next evolvement of the subject. The teaching today is too accelerated. It should be the other way around. There should not be classrooms with pupils in various learning ability categories. As nearly as possible, there should be classes with learners who are assimilating knowledge at the same rate of speed.

Ideally, there should be a teacher for each pupil. In this way is a clearer and more definite channel of communication established.

It is so easy to say that the learner is dense, or that the learner is stupid. This is not true at all in most instances. It is the teacher's inability to communicate to the learner—that is the problem. To communicate, a response has to be generated first with a preliminary clearing of the channel of communication. To clear the channel, the teacher must sweep out the mental blocks, emotional restraints, physical apprehensions, and clear away fears of one sort or another. Once confidence is established in the learner, then cooperation comes. Anger, irritability, all negative vibrations on either the teacher's or pupil's side create obstructions in the channel of communication.

February 16, 1960

If a teacher tries to reach his pupils' mentality, a corresponding echo will be evoked in his own mind and the force or impetus of the interchange in the channel will open the way for a clear communication link.

February 15, 1960

When a pupil understands that he will not be punished if he does not learn, but will be helped to learn, then will the profession of teaching become the art that it should be. Also, learning of subjects which are of no use to the pupil is definitely a waste of time and effort. In ages to come, each baby will have a horoscope drawn—when astrology reaches the point of being understood—and each teacher will receive the horoscope of each child, and also records of performance. This will enable the teacher to understand the pupils so that each pupil will be reached on his or her own channel of communication. The horoscopes will show which subjects should be taught to the pupils to prepare them for their own particular life's mission. The pupils will be enabled to practice the profession for which they had been created.

In God's plan for humanity, there is not one superfluous human being in the world. Each human is a cell in the body of humanity, and each cell has a job it was created to do. How few of these cells are really doing what they were created to do? This lack of knowledge by teachers is the root of many evils in society. Misfits and failures in society always evoke the picture of parents' failure in people's minds. This may not be the case at all. The failure most probably came from the teachers the individual had in his formative years. When this aspect of life is recognized and corrected there will be a sudden upswing in society's level of accomplishments in all fields.

Ultimately, each individual has to work with his own physical vehicle, but it is incumbent upon teachers to reach into the consciousness of their charges and help them fulfill their missions in life. This is a tremendous subject, no matter how one looks at it. Perhaps, the greatest single effort will be to teach humanity that it has a responsibility, one to another. To understand this intellectually is not enough. It is necessary to grasp this fact in the recesses of one's own being in order to practice it. How few realize this is tragic. Most individuals are caught in the web of lack of one sort or another, and that makes them grasping and selfish. A matter of survival, sometimes.

March 24, 1948

Responsibility only comes to the people able to cope with it. Breaking of ties always incurs more responsibility, because one becomes the owner of all the mistakes the ones left behind are continuing to commit.

It is never wise to rush ahead and do things without heeding the Christ within.

Knowledge, also, incurs a tremendous responsibility, because one becomes responsible for the use of the knowledge applied by those whom one taught. Here again, one should listen to the Christ within and teach only those who are ready to receive knowledge and to accept full responsibility for the results. Precious are the promptings of the Christ within the heart.

January 8, 1948

Great Souls find their work without much guidance or prompting. They are so constituted that they know at a glance. Just so, on Earth an inspired teacher uses discrimination of what to teach his pupils and is careful only to teach that which he knows his pupils can assimilate.

Sometimes intuition will tell what to talk about and what not to talk about. That is how Jesus taught.

March 22, 1948

Having brought teachings regarding conduct into the world, each such teacher becomes responsible for that part of humanity which follows his teachings. When their individual disciples in turn teach, they are responsible for the ones whom they have taught. Long ages pass, and still those disciples are bound to the Earth plane because they are teaching their former pupils the correct application of their teachings.

First, each teacher must be sure that the pupil is ready to assimilate the teachings he will give. This is important.

March 28, 1948

Many privileges are accorded Masters so that they may do their work more efficiently. Every help is given them.

Preparation for Mastership constitutes an entire change of the individual physically and spiritually. The mental body is complete and conscious. The physical body is conscious of the activities of the mental body. In a word, all bodies are conscious simultaneously. That is the meaning of Mastership.

January 11, 1948

When full realization comes, the man stands on two planes at once. He follows only the dictates of his God within. This takes form in many ways. He may teach, write, or work in another manner. Suffice it to say that he is contributing to the growth of humanity. The result is never of use to only the one achieving illumination. Many Great Souls work with others on like planes or come down to a lower plane to work directly with humanity. The work is ever one of service.

May 23, 1948

God sends teachers unto all peoples. Great and eternal truths are given to humanity always and in all ages. There is never a barren period on Earth when none of the truth is taught anywhere. There is someone in every land, in every nation, among every peoples, teaching the truth and passing on the flame.

In blessed lands there are many teachers and many groups, working for the spiritual unfoldment of humanity.

Jesus used parables.

August 22, 1948

Many years ago there dwelt in a far Northern land a man so old no one knew his age. Everyone had always remembered him. And then he disappeared. He never died. He is still living, being so perfect in body and soul that he is a real human. He teaches.

February 16, 1948

Many years of search by trial and error are required, as well as application of various tests before one can say that a soul is of the necessary caliber to take on the tremendous task of teaching. Man flings forth his challenge to the fates, who merely look at him and weave him into the pattern. What part he plays depends upon his rate of vibration.

December 18, 1947

God ordains certain individuals to be ministers to mankind. How this ministering will be demonstrated will depend in which stage of evolution is the individual. He may be a parent, physician, priest, teacher, and so forth. One fact remains: this kind of person will always be a little above the rest. This is because these individuals' souls emanated from a certain ray, which has its own characteristics. Call this ray Elohim if you like.

This ray proceeds from beyond Aquarius, works its way through to the Earth, and manifests in a peculiar type of individual. These are recognized by their light; it vibrates a longer wave than that of the ordinary aura, and the astral image is half again as large as the ordinary. Only a few of these dwell on Earth. That is the origin of the Chosen People legend. You may call these Is-Real-ites.

March 15, 1949

Many souls show forth a wondrous beam, and this beam must be cultivated. It must be a result of right thinking and also right living.

February 16, 1948

Good is that which raises the vibrations nearer the dazzling white light. Evil is that which lessens it toward grossness. Since man's place is in the white light, grossness is painful. Why did man sink into matter? He sought to gain knowledge of it, to enrich his experience, and to redeem it.

This is an addition to God's creation, since we are part of Him.

Moses' Decalogue lives to point the way to raising vibrations; also, Jesus' Sermon on the Mount does this. Zarathustra's teachings are a guidepost.

March 15, 1949

If there is any doubt or fear, instead of faith and confidence, that soul will not shine or emanate any color.

July 20, 1960

When civilization was in its infancy, the leaders held a conclave to decide upon a method of teaching truths that would not be too difficult. Reason was simple; memory was short; needs were basic. Early man was more an animal than human, but that spark of soul was there, and that made all the difference between man and animal. The need of man was to cultivate that spark to be a suffusing throughout his being. So shall it be for the entire race of man.

February 19, 1948

From the beginning of the world's creation, Great Ones were marked as teachers and guides of humanity. Additional Great Ones made the sacrifice to take on bodies and to help with the task. Humanity's problems are leading to chaos, and stabilizing forces such as Great Souls are needed to keep the balance.

June 9, 1948

Humanity must acquire experience and knowledge to add beauty and color to God's creation. Many will get the highest knowledge and propound the truth to those who follow.

February 22, 1949

A necessity to true comprehension is deep study. Slowly man brings his hidden potentialities to light and unfolds like a chrysalis to a much greater and truer existence, of which this is but an empty shadow. But one rule of unfoldment and development mandates that aid to be given to others so that they may at least start on the way to unfoldment and the new way of life. A crowning effect is the full development of the head centers. Incidentally, that is the true meaning of a crown on a king. The points signify the rays emanating from the head centers of an Illumined One.

In ancient times people were simpler, but more comprehending. Because of this simplicity, they could plainly see the superiority of such a being and understand the meaning of the crown.

February 23, 1948

All the most high and esoteric teaching is never written; it is transmitted by word of mouth, from teacher to pupil. Such generalities, as can be given, have been given to humanity since the beginning of time. All that can be done now is to keep modernizing it to fit the understanding of humanity in its advanced stage of development.

Long years of practice are required to even do one little thing correctly. It will not be easy to lead a totally new life. No one hands over an individual to an idea, or to an ideal, but his own inner compulsion.

March 3, 1949

Bringing forth wisdom to guide others is one of the greatest tasks which man must do to help others. Whoever answers this call and fulfills it, can know great joy and will acquire boundless wisdom if that is his goal.

March 31, 1949

What an individual knows and passes on, ten times that amount is given him. He loves humanity in its spiritual aspect and not in its material form. There is a difference.

August 23, 1950

God blesses all who put their time at the disposal of the Lord. When souls dedicate themselves to God, they are taught almost immediately. Although they are unaware of being taught, their instruction goes forward on the spiritual plane.

March 4, 1960

The beauty of life is an endowed thing. The guiding Brothers help one to overcome problems, and life becomes smooth. Often this happens unbeknownst to the recipient of this aid.

September 11, 1961

Welfare of Initiates is always of uppermost importance to the Great Ones. They are always in touch to keep track of things as they are. When the young ones, especially, need help, this is extended immediately. Long ago, this physical welfare was none of their concern, but now things have changed and are different. Things have developed at such a rapid pace that it is necessary to help in the physical sense, too. This is understood and acted upon at last.

May 16, 1948

Small rewards are the rewards of small deeds. The deed of showing the laws of God is the greatest that can be accomplished, and you will grow the greater for your dissemination of truth. Follow inspiration.

February 7, 1948

Proper language is needed to reach each individual. Not every human will respond to the same words and phrases, and too much cannot be written to develop man along spiritual lines.

All men must learn to rely on the guide within.

March 23, 1949

Bring forth your concept of the eternal and people will laugh. They do not understand that which cannot be demonstrated on the objective, three-dimensional plane of being.

If one more dimension were added, then all would be permanent, but that is not possible on this plane.

March 23, 1949

Lacking a convenient yardstick, they measure success by material possessions and accumulation of goods. They always lose sight of the impermanence of this state of being and having. It is only the soul qualities that one acquires which are permanent. All else is as nothing.

February 19, 1960

Probably the greatest deterrent to the study of the soul by the public is lack of interest in the inner life. The general attitude of the public is—"What's in it for Me?" Also there are individuals whom in their whole lives have never had a single psychic experience, a single significant dream. After all, there must be some way to create a personal interest and desire for the study of the inner life and its potential in order to realize that potentiality. Is it possible to create an alignment in an individual from the outside, so that the individual will have a desire to look into and study mysticism?

There is nothing like a personal experience and a personal knowledge. When one has that, no one can take it away and it does not vanish with the retelling. Therefore, one way to combat any lethargy by the public is to work at helping people have more inner experiences and visions. Then they, themselves, will know that there is a kingdom of God. Teachers of mankind, hear this.

December 31, 1947

Many Great Souls wish not to experience incarnation, yet want knowledge of life conditions upon this planet. They lower their vibrations enough to contact a highly evolved soul and gain much knowledge of conditions by following the life of the terrestrial dweller.

They are allowed to help humanity evolve faster in this way, because the presence of these Beings automatically raises the vibrations of those near them. The effect, if continued often, becomes permanent.

God wills that at this time a great influx of highly vibrating Beings people the Earth for a while to counterbalance man's evil creations, which are enough already to destroy the world. Man must destroy these evils himself while he learns his lessons through their effect on him.

Great things will humanity accomplish at this time because of these Beings' presence, which has raised vibrations and heightened intuition.

Beings such as these gain vast knowledge through this experience, and this association is mutually beneficial. But for their presence, the world would surely be destroyed through man's machinations.

When in contact with one of these Beings, the effect on humans is a slightly elated condition, a swaying of the astral body. Their knowledge encompasses conditions unexplainable to man, but as much as man will understand is freely given.

Small wonder that esoteric groups have been springing up rapidly. Each individual who receives an inspiration will want to share it and will gather a sympathetic group about him. If the group is strong enough psychically and their collective vibration high enough, they will attract at least one Great Soul to teach and inspire them. An international group will have scores of Great Souls helping it. It all works out to the mutual advantage of everyone.

March 3, 1948

Only the greatest souls know how to arrange their lives properly. Even so, they cannot escape utterly some vicissitudes of living in the flesh. These souls have taken on bodies voluntarily to act as teachers and guides of humanity. Their task is thankless. People learn only under and by compulsion. This compulsion may be their own sorrow or irksome circumstances, or an imposition of a superior's will.

The teachers learn by intuition and also by lessons learned on the inner planes.

March 15, 1948

Preparation for a teaching role takes many centuries. The teacher is taught by various souls of the Hierarchy, and then is helped constantly while on the Earth plane. A curious fact is that each teacher, without exception, begged humanity not to worship him, but to regard God and worship Him, instead.

Friends are the only religious body which observes this scrupulously. Many messengers did God send to obviate this tendency of mankind to idolatry by remaining anonymous or doing their work without fanfare.

Preparation, prayers and unswerving will are basic requirements for this type of ministry.

Lowering of vibrations to incarnate in a body, so that it will not fly to pieces at contact, takes about three centuries. This amount of time seems long to humanity, but actually it is a very short while.

April 3, 1948

God is the prime mover and governor of the universe. Problems of old times are the problems of today, because humanity has not evolved sufficiently to understand the workings of the law of the universe. Those who do understand, leave the Earth plane and advance to a higher form of creation, which itself is evolving to a still higher form of being. Given opportunities, man still hesitates to lift his consciousness toward spirituality.

What is the difference between spirituality and materiality as far as man is concerned? When man lives in the material world he is, of course, governed by the laws of the material plane. He functions in only three dimensions. Should he sink still lower, he will function in only two dimensions, and we know of it as the sphere of fire or hell. Man's sinking to all the lower spheres from his original seventh plane, where he functions in seven dimensions, is all very unnatural for him. That is why he suffers so much. The higher man goes toward his home in the seventh heaven, as it were, the less suffering he experiences. Our immediate concern is to advance to the next higher spiritual plane, where man functions in four dimensions. Of the fourth we know everything; that is, those of us who have attained that state of consciousness.

Of the fifth we know a good deal. Of the sixth, we have inklings.

And of the seventh, we only surmise.

The law governing man's advance to his immediate higher plane is the law of love. When one loves even physically, one moves in a roseate world of one's own creation. When one attains a perpetual state of the emotion and includes all creatures in creation, humanity, animals, and plant life, then he has attained Mastership. To such a one all doors are open.

July 5, 1960

We have watched the affairs of men for centuries. In fact, we are called the Silent Watchers. One of us, in turn, stands at the opening of the cone of darkness to prevent evil from coming in.

September 3, 1960

We only observe what is happening in the world and can look ahead to see outcomes of various events. This is quite important to know, but it does not change the course of history. It is not in our power to do so. Yes, there have been three times that we know of when the course of history was changed. That was to save some remnants of the human race on Earth. The noble experiments which have been going on are still going on in shaping and unfolding man to his full true potential. And his full true potential is something you cannot imagine. It is so breathtakingly glorious as to beggar description. You will catch a glimpse of this far distant time a little later, and will realize why it is necessary for man to go through these periods of trial and tribulation so that he will learn to grow in the true manner.

We watch and we pray constantly. When we see where humanity is wending, we pray that they will take the right turning and evolve in the right manner. Oh, yes, the three events when the Brotherhood changed the course of history—in Atlantis, in Egypt during the Napoleonic wars, and on the plains of Middle Europe in battle when men met to repulse the Muslims in Europe during invasion by Turks. With our help, under direction of intelligences beyond your understanding, the course of history was changed. Eventually the same ends would have been reached, but very much delayed. Things were speeded up a little, but they are still behind what they should have been.

Chapter Seven

▼

Discipleship

March 20, 1948

Many people prepare themselves for an active life of preaching the laws which raise the soul's vibrations to such an extent that the individual awakens on the spiritual plane as well as on the physical.

March 31, 1949

When individuals know various laws of daily living and follow them, definite spiritual growth occurs. The mental body evolves and becomes fully conscious.

March 20, 1948

It is a fact that when the body lies down in sleep the psychic one should step forth, fully conscious, and proceed, swiftly as an arrow, to the Hall of Learning, where it receives instructions for still higher vibrations. This Hall of Learning is still a physical place, just as the psychic body is still a physical being.

July 11, 1948

Consciousness is the realization of self as a living, functioning part of creation. It is an attribute of soul. Only those who desire with their whole hearts a union with God, are raising their vibrations sufficiently to attract aid from the Invisible Host of Teachers and Helpers. Persons living without aspirations betray their heritage.

Who calls above and scorns worldly aspirations will achieve eternal life.

God knows His own and calls them His own in no unmistakable terms. Firmness of purpose is highly essential to advancement, as is perseverance.

February 7, 1948

God prepares various souls to do various types of work. These are led along the lines they will follow by doing the preparatory work on this plane.

Firmness of purpose is a necessary development to advancement of the spiritual man. He develops single-mindedness, which is a necessary requirement to create. Slow, even development, is better than spasmodic sudden spurts. Easily and slowly the individual advances until he has the necessary strength to cope with the new problems he has grown into.

February 20, 1949

"Seek and ye shall find" is no idle command. It applies to everything. When a human being decides to attain some goal, he consciously and subconsciously works only toward that goal. He creates it in the world of ideas and brings it into being on the material plane. He does what God did in creating. This power of creating is a unique endowment of humanity.

February 11, 1948

Principally, the one virtue which develops the soul fastest is steadfastness of purpose. This teaches the art of concentration and visualization which is so important to creating. If one is swayed often by circumstances and people, one develops a vacillating will which retards development.

March 9, 1960

Control of self is fine, but then there are times when one must act. It is the times when to act, and when not to act, that one must use one's intelligence and discrimination. There are many such decisions that a human being makes every day—some are important and some are not. The main thing is that the great game of life must go on. If we make mistakes and learn by that, then the mistakes have done some good and have served their purpose. No matter how much or how little one knows—it is through making some effort in some direction that one learns more, even if it is a mistake and one learns what not to do. The business of learning goes on forever.

February 11, 1948

Love is the surest emotion of all in developing the soul, because of its constancy. Single-minded application builds, but vacillation of purpose is disruptive.

March 6, 1949

Many problems confront an individual when he sets his foot upon the path of spiritual attainment. One who has achieved Mastership is no longer subject to others' whims; he can order his life to best advantage by his knowledge of natural laws.

A problem of aspirants is that of not liking that form of amusement and entertainment which his companions previously provided. He will see the shallowness and emptiness of most public entertainment. He will see things as they really are and mock the utter futility of his former companions' pursuits. His whole circle of friends will gradually change and will be replaced by ones thinking similarly as he does.

He will learn to control his thoughts. That is the primary step to spiritual attainment. The ability to control thought is the greatest achievement of man. Thoughts are as unreined wild steeds darting wherever and however they wish; but once they are harnessed by the individual and directed, the step is taken in the right direction. Incidentally, that is the most difficult task of the aspirant to Mastership.

February 9, 1948

Skill in expression is invaluable as far as letters are concerned. Many have been the awakenings of self simply through correspondence. Great achievements have gone forth because of letters. Symbols are for those who have gone to the heights of such understanding that they can read a volume by looking at a symbol. But for one who can do this there are countless millions who cannot. That is why it is necessary to acquire extreme facility of expression and a thorough knowledge of symbols.

September 12, 1960

True perspective can only be attained and achieved at the cost of personal bias and point of view. A relatively true perspective can be achieved, but it takes a rare personality to accomplish this. In fact, so rare are they that there are barely a half dozen in any given century of time that are in incarnation. Their perspective manifests in daily living and may not be making earthshaking history. Nevertheless, all individuals contacting these rare and unusual individuals have had their lives immeasurably enriched, yes, enriched to the point of enabling the individual to take strides in his or her own evolvement.

July 19, 1960

Billions of years have passed since the dawn of creation, as we know time, so look how long it takes man to civilize himself. The process is still going on. How long it takes to civilize the average man is anybody's guess. The souls who took the quick path have forty-nine lives to live and develop from probationer to Initiate. It is a hard and difficult process, and not to be recommended to everyone. The life of a probationer is especially hard, because the animal part of man is so firmly entrenched in the consciousness and inner being. It involves a constant watchfulness and an ever-present application of mental processes to the conduct of affairs in a particular way. Ethics become very important. An ethical life is a very difficult life to lead. Long years of sincere effort are needed to make an ethical life possible. The return of a particular cycle in the world's history makes the idea of ethics very important at certain times.

February 1, 1960

Conduct is very important in the world of men and also in a spiritual sense. What one is, essentially, will inevitably be reflected in one's conduct. Kindness must manifest itself and consideration of one's fellow man, and these not only on the surface, but within. This is an acquired attribute. Man in the raw is extremely unkind to others, and the consideration aspect is absent altogether. But, as this is developed, there occurs a change in one's inner being and true humanity is born. Whether it lasts is the individual's problem. Periods get longer and longer as one practices these things, and then one is always kind and considerate. Lapses get rarer and rarer, until finally they vanish altogether.

February 28, 1949

When progress of soul is intended in any one life, the individual leads a varied existence. His life is not of the humdrum variety in some quiet little community. An inner compulsion sends him into circumstances, if not into environments, which will provide opportunity for that soul's progress. What an individual is and what he does is decided by himself alone. Up to a certain point, an ego is guided by his guardian angel, as it were, but there comes a time when he must take his destiny into his own hands and mold himself. Relatively few are such Masters of their own destiny, but many are on the way.

In many ways, an ego resembles a shadow which follows an individual and is passively absorbing the experiences of the physical part. As the influence of the physical lessens, the strength and full functioning of the ego occurs. One grows at the expense of the other. As life in the flesh lessens, life in the spirit increases. An even balance is always maintained between the two.

The power which makes all things possible is "Christ."

March 1, 1949

All good men are Chosen Ones' no matter creed, race, or color. Each individual must experience incarnation in many diverse forms. Therefore, it is folly to say that one is better than the other. None are better. Only some are of a higher vibration. What an individual needs to realize is that he must try to raise his vibrations, work to open his centers, and live in Christ or have Christ live in him, if you prefer.

So many individuals know of this and continue to live their own lives of selfish animosity toward everyone and everything except the gratification of their own senses. Such people are like the foolish virgins who trim not their lamps. They do learn some lessons in their incarnations, because no life is without its lesson, but very little progress is made.

An ideal life is the full realization of all its potentialities, as shown in a natal chart. This chart shows all an individual has to learn and what he has to overcome, and how much progress he has to make. Most individuals conform to this, changing some aspects only slightly.

May 10, 1960

Long-range plans sometimes do not work because they do not serve our best interests. Very simple. Conditions vary with each new set of actions, and some conditions may not be necessary to our soul's evolvement. We only do the things and experience the experiences which are necessary for us. There is a wonderful economy about our lives. Nothing is ever lost.

November 11, 1954

When a disciple is showing signs of advancement, he is helped in every way possible. Tests and trials are arranged to see if the disciple can be helped in any way to advance. All help is extended, but the disciple is seldom aware of the help he is receiving. In fact, it is better that he should not know. All advancement will then seem to come from the disciple's own efforts. And the disciples are protected. Even in circumstances when they think they are alone, they are protected.

February 11, 1948

Lacking self-discipline, most people make a mess of their lives. They become influenced by error and thus do wrong things.

Certain of the Great Souls who guide the affairs of humanity protect the Chosen Ones (who chose themselves) from following the prompting of error. Many people show their Discipleship to error by willfully following pursuits which lessen their vibratory rate.

Symbolically, these people are known as squares. They can only achieve perfection upon building a pyramid of their lives upon the square base.

And a pyramid is composed of triangles. Man cannot get away from attaining perfection, because this is the law.

February 8, 1949

God loves Great Souls who do His work willingly, learn His laws and apply them to the least of daily functions to establish harmony and peace in the world.

Shall many or the few rule the world? It depends upon which ones serve God and thus fulfill their mission.

February 25, 1948

People are led by visible creation to a better understanding of God's laws as manifested on Earth. From there, the laws governing the spiritual world can readily be deduced. Following a pattern to its beginnings is a good method of realizing how laws operate. All Great Souls must know these laws and work according to them to maintain an even balance.

March 3, 1949

Sweet are the angel voices when one more soul attains Discipleship. It brings more harmony into the world which sorely needs it. Probably the thing most needed in the world today is such understanding which will cause brotherhood. Where there is no understanding, there is either indifference or strife. Both do not make for progress.

June 4, 1948

The greatest good to the greatest number come freely from God; the only thing required is an active intelligent will to direct it. When joy is manifested, there you find inspiration at work and a sincere desire to be of service.

The criterion of high evolvement is not knowledge. It is humility, and the degree to which the individual possesses it.

June 7, 1948

Come to the heavenly kingdom in humility, and in no other way. Success on this Earth plane is unimportant in heaven. Only those deeds count which contribute to spiritual growth.

April 19, 1948

All things belong to God and not to men. Emulation of men who talk and live righteousness is good. All souls must be prepared to step forward to reach righteousness. Many souls can tell what to do, but are unable to make their own vehicles obey their will. All are blessed who are about their Lord's business. He allows small inconveniences to build strength of character and an unswerving will. Conditions vary, that make a person strong. Some people gain strength through peace and calm, and some gain it only by adversity. God knows of which ray one is and the means of evolution, functioning automatically, enables an individual to gain strength.

June 1, 1948

The way and method stand before each man for his choice. He must choose whether he wants to progress to spirituality or not. He may not be conscious of this in his physical body, but the cycle of evolution proceeds whether man wishes to cooperate or not.

His love of fleshly ease and opulence is the worst drawback to his evolvement. Dissatisfaction is the best spur to evolvement.

December 15, 1947

In a state when the individual accepts everything and changes its vibration to a better state, is the mystery of correct living. It consists of the transmutation of events and even occurrences of worldwide importance into a vibration of that particular intensity which will lift humanity out of density into its true home.

That is why some individuals are selected to head nations, communities, and groups. If these become willing, obedient instruments of the Brethren working for humanity's good, they are of great benefit not only to their countries but to the world.

April 22, 1948

Only those whose motives are entirely selfless whose actions are based on the good and blessing of all are fit to do the work of the Brothers. This work is stupendous. It concerns the awakening of man's senses to a life of fullness in God. Heretofore, man developed his material intellect to such an extent that he is ready to become aware of the divine purpose and scheme as far as he is concerned.

February 29, 1948

God follows the highest source of good. Only men of great wisdom will understand this. Unfathomable to the average human mind is this vast source. Resurrection of souls rises periodically to this source of all good. They go to the highest heaven.

Many souls on Earth today are being harvested for heaven and they are unaware of it. God looks after His own always.

The slightest turning toward Him is known.

God lets His own provide for themselves but will lead them toward what they desire.

February 10, 1949

Will human beings ever know wisdom? Yes, but only when people seek wisdom and learn the futility of possessions in the material sense. So will humanity advance spiritually when it transmutes its desires to a higher plane.

Many years ago the human race provided for itself simply, but exigencies of civilization compel a more complicated existence today.

June 8, 1948

Although trials and tribulations wash the face of the Earth, the blessed ones need have no fear. These are taken care of and never suffer. The ones meeting adversity go through the purifying process.

Service September 14, 1960

What kind of life does a person lead who is almost never in touch with the affairs of the world of men? Useless, that's what. Usefulness to himself alone is very selfish. One cannot live for self alone. One must live for others, as well. An individual's worth can be gauged by his influence on others. The better the influence, the better the person. However, there may be a selfish motive for doing good, but that will show itself.

July 30, 1960

God ordains that all who dedicate their lives in service to humanity, dedicate their lives in service to Him. This service may take any form applicable to the evolvement of being on any plane of endeavor. This can be extended to kindness to all kingdoms. The only stipulation is that there is no selfish motive.

June 5, 1960

In essence, the allotted task of life is to render service. One must learn lessons which enrich and ennoble the soul. Also, one must help others to achieve these same ends. That is the real purpose of life. If everyone lived that kind of life, we would not have any more worries in the world. And people who achieve this, achieve the most benefit out of their incarnations.

January 27, 1948

Real living consists of service, but, mind you, service which spiritualizes the ones who contact you. No nobler life can be possible.

Many individuals think they are doing good when they spend their material wealth on poverty-stricken individuals. Usually, the ones who accept charity are lazy, ambitionless, hardened individuals, who are belligerently demanding support. This sort of service does not do any good. Only the kind which regenerates individuals and teaches them to be unselfish is of the greatest benefit.

There is enough of everything in the world to take care of everyone. Unfortunately for some, it requires work.

February 21, 1949

Inexorable working rules decree that man must work. All must work. If someone does not work, it is because he has gained the consent of someone else to do his share of the work. When one is born into riches and freedom from want, he should still work at something, not gainfully necessarily, but something which will benefit the greatest number. Many wealthy people are such pillars of charitable institutions. They are fulfilling the decree regarding work and are doing service to humanity also.

In some respects this work for work's sake is a greater blessing and brings greater satisfaction than the work performed very grudgingly by someone who has to work for a living. Very few love their work enough never to complain at the necessity of doing it. A happy and cheerful worker is a blessed one. His work is blessed also.

May 1, 1948

Only those who persevere with earnest application will do any good to others, and also to themselves. When humanity learns that the best way to help self is to help others, the greatest step in evolution will have taken place. One of the principle laws of the universe is service.

When one does not exact payment for one's service, one leaves the gate open for cosmic repayment in all the fullness thereof. When humanity understands this corollary, there will no longer be poverty and privation.

January 15, 1948

There is much more in the cosmic storehouse than has been dispensed. The only requisite for distribution is one of service. Therefore, the more we do for others; the more we ourselves can receive in return.

One must live by the words of Jesus because that is the way to reintegration with God. Perhaps, the greatest single factor to spiritual growth is unselfishness. The more one lives only for self and in oneself, the more one shuts off the source of good.

Great things are expected of great people. When the proper time comes, the greatness is allowed to come through for the benefit of all.

When individuals allow themselves to think of naught else but themselves, their vision is shut off from all other effects which are of great benefit to themselves. God established this law before many others.

February 27, 1949

Many people build a too solid barrier between themselves and humanity, and that prevents them from fulfilling the law of helping humanity. An individual progresses only as much as he helps another progress.

March 7, 1948

Probably the greatest thing man can do, is to help others without thought of self. Living is a hard task, but forging ahead in a given field must be attended with prayerful intentness of purpose. God helps everyone who dedicates his work to Him.

February 2, 1948

Greatness of soul and spirit spells achievement as far as terrestrial life is concerned. And this greatness can be determined by how much one gives of one's life to the upliftment of one's fellow man and asks nothing in return. Growth and development under Earth conditions are extremely difficult, because so much time and effort are required to keep the body functioning properly. With some, it is a full-time effort which leaves no time to develop the soul. One is helped constantly by unseen guides and angels who inspire and teach. Following of one's intuition is still the surest way of doing the right thing. That is the only way the soul can direct the body in an untrained individual.

February 27, 1949

What is a universal law? This pertains to spiritual progress on the inner planes but works on the material plane as well.

What can one do to help others progress? One can be civil when approached and helpful with suggestions for greater mental progress. Where can one meet these people? They will come to one.

March 18, 1949

Many will come psychically to be helped. That is the work which counts. That is the true service, when souls come for advice and help and it is given them. That is when the greatest help is given and is known as "Let not thy right hand know what thy left hand doeth." One may live an entirely hermit-like existence, yet be out helping humanity advance. That is one of the greatest truths of the universe.

The service a physical body renders is but a poor shadow of that on the inner planes.

A true meaning of hypocrisy is that of a do-gooder rushing around on the physical plane helping everyone and being entirely selfish about helping others advance spiritually.

December 24, 1947

Ownership of property and worldly goods does not constitute Mastership. On the other hand, complete poverty is a hindrance to development. We have to use the world's goods to imbue them with higher vibrations.

The happy medium of accepting what the natural gifts may be and using them to the best advantage is true service. No, do not scorn wealth and its appurtenances.

First glimpses of a spiritual life are so wonderful because they are so foreign to the material self. The task is to blend the two and spiritualize the body. This is not a difficult thing to do. All that is necessary is to learn to listen to the One within for all instructions, whether the instructions are regarding material or spiritual things. In that way, one can fulfill the tasks and lessons set forth in each life. A right listening will result in joyous living. It is only when we do not listen that we reap heartache and sorrow.

October 18, 1955

Obligation and fulfillment are two different things. Man may obligate himself to do a certain thing, but his vehicle may not be up to the task. Sometimes the work is held in abeyance until the consciousness of the being evolves a sufficiently capable vehicle.

May 12, 1948

Whomsoever God has chosen to do His allotted tasks, that individual is blessed beyond all imagination. It is a hard path to travel, this being the Servant of the Lord, but it is most satisfying.

November 11, 1954

The reason humanity learns so slowly from experience, and why the same mistakes are made repeatedly, is that individuals cannot interpret experience unless they know their own symbology or law of being.

When individuals start to know themselves, the next logical step which follows is to see where they fit into the cultural pattern as it manifests in humanity as a whole.

Thus the steps which are being taken every time experiences are met, will either lead up to expanded consciousness, or to a repetition of the same experience in another guise to learn the lesson presented by the experience.

When considering where all fit into the scheme of things, it leads to the general cultural and historical function of Christianity. It considers the cultural structure as it has manifested down through the ages in human society. This must be done to find one's rightful place and function in the social organization.

Once we know who and what we are, we must study the pattern which humanity is weaving, so that the thread of our life will be one of gold, as it were.

Symbols are useful as illustrations. A simple one which is familiar to all which can be used to illustrate the body of humanity is the pyramid.

A pyramid stands on a square base, containing many, many stones. Each face of the pyramid is a triangle, and each succeeding line of stones reaching toward the top contains less stones as the pyramid tapers toward the top. This can be used as an analogy, so that each line of stones has individuals of varying unfoldment of consciousness, intellectual ability and spirituality. Even as each line has less and less stones, so does each strata of society, as it evolves higher toward reality, toward full flowering as a real image of divinity—in fact, what it was created to be in the image of God with full powers. The numbers of these individuals become fewer and fewer, as one proceeds higher. Now, in that vast pyramid of humanity, each individual has an own rightful place. And this is the tragedy of mankind: very few individuals are in their rightful places in that pyramid of humanity. Most of them go through life with the feeling of "suffer it to be so for now"—this is just temporary—but, some day—! However, some day never comes and whole lives are lived with that feeling of temporariness in professions, in communities, belonging to wrong groups, and so on. First, study the pattern that the social order takes. In sheer numbers, we find the entirely material people. Their whole aim in life is to live in the senses, and for the satisfaction of the senses. They live to feed themselves, adorn themselves and to propagate.

Those in the next higher strata live in the senses, too, but emotion plays a great part in their lives. They are good people, and some can live wonderfully exemplary lives, lives of sacrifice for others, loving kind—but their lives lack direction. When moved by their emotions they mount the steed of their good intentions and gallop off in all directions, dissipating the greater amount of their energy, using the lesser amount of it.

Then there are the thinkers, those that have direction. In the last group, the ones toward the apex of the pyramid, one finds what they all have in common. It spells out service. The products of their labors are such that they contribute to the betterment of society in some manner, shape, or form. Their work will be of a nature that helps others in difficulties, in some way. Even as there are outside stones in each layer of a pyramid, with at least one face not receiving any pressure and is open to the Sun, so the lowliest scrub woman in the pyramid of the social structure, who may live a life of uncomplaining service, can be likened to an outside stone, though her inner unfoldment is very slight and intellectual achievements, nil.

One thing stands out: the lower one is in the pyramid, the greater the pressure on all sides, and the less opportunity to get out of it.

February 9, 1960

God needs willing workers in His vineyard to accomplish His plans for evolvement of everything on Earth, not only of man but even of minerals. Things advance in the scale of their own being, too. Man is an expression of God, but there are other expressions. All is evolving toward a common goal, which is unity with God. A big mystery of existence is the reason for this Will of God to create the universe and everything in it. There must be a purpose behind all this law and order and grand concept which comprises the universe and everything in it. It would be incomprehensible if there was so much expression of purposeful action and great energy but not purpose. There must be purpose, and man will be allowed to discover it.

March 5, 1948

All men can attain knowledge and Mastership in one lifetime if they will but apply themselves to the process. Distinct success would mark their efforts. God does not withhold, ever.

Follow directions as set forth in the Decalogue and in the Sermon on the Mount and you will do God's work among men.

The nature of good is that which raises the vibrations of an individual and spiritualizes him. Good consists of constructive effort toward the Godhead.

Probably the most good in the world is done by people who strive to help others without thought of raising their own vibrations or hoping for a reward. These people are not conscious of self. Therefore, they are unselfish. Their vibrations are unbelievably high. They shine.

Chapter Eight

Organizations and Orders

Group Work   December 18, 1947

Whatever man elects to do, he either consecrates the deed to the glorification of God or of self. When the deed is for the glory of God, it blesses all; and whomever it touches, that individual's vibrations will be raised, if only temporarily. No matter how humble is the task, the results can be noble.

Man keeps the keys to the heavenly kingdom in his own grasp. The St. Peter in each person admits him to the higher plane of existence. This is wholly reasonable. If a person's rate of vibration is heightened, he advances in spite of himself. And the beauty of one individual's raising of vibrations is that he raises those with whom he comes in contact. The slower, grosser people may resent this, and an unexplained antipathy may arise.

Consequently, group work is very important. Not only do these people help themselves but they charge the very atmosphere. This draws into the group those souls which respond to these vibrations. The aphorism, "Birds of a feather flock together," is an explanation of a truth, as most sayings seem to be.

Man heeds prompting of inner compulsion only when he has successfully subdued the powerful clamor of the physical self. Association with people whose physical selves serve the soul is, therefore, important to beginners on the path. And for this reason group work is highly essential. Just the mere contact helps the beginner, and sustains the advanced one. Strong indeed are the vibrations of one who walks amid the grosser forces of humanity and keeps renewing from within his own vibrations as fast as they are depleted by the people around him.

What builds these vibrations? Kindness of purpose, thought, and action do this. Thought is most important, because man creates with his thoughts. It matters very much what a person thinks, because he exudes waves from his head continually. And these thoughts bunch together and create airy forms. If the thoughts are strong and constant enough, they will materialize and have physical forms. This is what is meant by wish-fulfillment.

February 12, 1949

Laws are the same throughout the universe. Different aspects of it are manifested, that is all. Aspects of life shadow forth universal truths. One does not need interstellar journeying or extended sight and hearing to comprehend God's universe. Not at all—everything is around him and in him. All he needs to do is study and meditate upon self to comprehend everything.

Some will spout forth the necessity for special study, breathing and meditation. Some of these are in impossible places to which one must travel. If a person applies himself to leading a good, clean life, he will be led to groups studying along mystical lines. He will learn that nothing he has not known already will be told to him. Only it will be the little things which have not come to his attention because they seemed so commonplace and unimportant, but he will learn that there is an aspect to them which illustrates a cosmic truth.

December 27, 1947

Blending of auras when two individuals are in close proximity can be advantageous to both people if there is only the roseate hued of love in the nimbus. But the muddy swirling of anger and despondency or fear can be irksome to a highly vibrating soul if it contacts those negative vibrations too frequently.

When individuals come into meetings of groups, it is important that they do not bring their troubles and anxieties with them. They must come in with pure thought. Their cares and burdens should be left at the threshold. Through an influx of Divine Wisdom at the meetings with others, when their vibrations are lifted, perhaps permanently, they will find an inspiration about how to dissolve their cares and anxieties.

Especially is it true of meetings in fraternal organizations. The sometimes unrecognized purpose of these organizations is to prepare individuals to take their place in the Great White Lodge in the cosmic. Also, these meetings are for raising one's vibrations to that degree where one's soul will guide one in the arrangement of everyday affairs. One's thoughts and actions should be a constant blessing and be motivated by love. It is difficult with some self-engrossed individuals, but that is the only way to growth. A glowing outpouring of love is the greatest burner-up of animal desires and emotions. And this can be achieved only through the possession of the twelve virtues. Great indeed is the soul which can achieve it in one incarnation.

The greater the achievement of this glow, the more animal individuals will be burned and their emotions turn to hate. Care must be taken to understand this process and of forgiving these sudden haters, because we actually make them suffer.

We agitate their solar plexuses, which are the seat of the animal passions, and they have not learned to respond to the heart, which is the abode of the spirit.

December 22, 1947

Slow degrees of vibration do not necessarily impede the flow of Divine Wisdom. The receiver assimilates, digests and sets forth as much of the truth as he can comprehend. Many greatly learned are of slow vibration. It depends from which ray the individual emanated. One must not be impatient with people of slower thought processes. They are still true members of the group. Many of the greatest workers have been these steadfast plodding individuals. If they do display lack of brilliancy in their intellect by your standards, it is only because they are of a different rate of vibration. In time it will be raised to equal yours. Sincerity of purpose and a willingness to work unrewarded are the virtues you must look for.

God's ways to lead mankind to His kingdom are twelve. Within the group are twelve kinds of individuals, each typifying a way to God. The twelve? Patience, kindness, willingness to work without reward, tolerance, continence, piety, devotion to an ideal, dedication of self to God's work among men, love and earnest pursuit of wisdom, greatness of heart to understand and alleviate suffering, and pure love. The last is Mastership. As each is the embodiment of one of the above virtues, he is still an exponent of varying degree of the other virtues. Together they constitute the body of an organization.

Organizations February 16, 1948

Divine Mind always gives great inner compulsions to right long-felt wrongs through Orders and organizations flung worldwide. These prepare souls to teach humanity.

December 15, 1947

God ordains organizations to carry on the work of man's regeneration. This work includes men and women in all walks of life. When an organization starts working, usually it is investigated by one of the Brethren and a fit vehicle is selected to transmit some truths which will create new trends in thought, thereby raising the vibrations of the members. This is what ordinarily happens. However, when an organization is an initiatory body which works toward the creation of Masters, it must receive the ever constant guidance, help and inspiration from a Great Teacher. Great truths will emerge from and find expression in the group, and this will serve as an inspiration to many other organizations in the world. God wills an utter, valiant, strong effort at this time to lift humanity into a higher plane of vibration. Preaching pretty words is useless, and work is necessary to point the example of fine results from right living. Such is the goal of all officers of esoteric organizations. They must set the example of their lives so that others can pattern their behavior upon those of the few Chosen Ones.

July 24, 1948

All brothers are members of one body. The whole will suffer if one is not applying self wholeheartedly and with pure intent to the task at hand. This is especially true of organizations and societies of an esoteric nature, members of which are more sensitive and attuned, one to another. A finely attuned group can do much good work in the world to help mankind. From all such groups, when combined, a great force of vibration pours forth to quicken humanity. Preparation of self for great work entails great efforts. A steadfast application of all rules set forth in the teachings must be applied or the member fails in his obligations, and consequently draws much suffering to himself.

Not all good souls of olden times, even saints, are on spiritual planes or are great Initiates. They flee from incarnation but cannot rise higher for lack of spiritual qualities. In fact, members of esoteric societies teach them in projection on this plane and on higher planes during sleep.

A question arises: Why do high degree members of esoteric Orders suffer physical disabilities, have operations, and so on? First, one must consider the term "high" as applied to degree of development. A standing of high degree on this plane does not always indicate the true spiritual degree to which the individual has progressed. Since this plane is the plane of lies and deception, anyone assuming a sanctimonious mien and mouthing high-sounding phrases can pass themselves off as a veritable saint. On the inner plane, however, where even thoughts are visible, this is not possible. Therefore, the term "high degree" must be used advisedly.

February 6, 1948

An entity of 100 degrees on the inner planes is a Savior. Some of these are Jesus, Osiris, Lao-Tse, Brahma, Buddha, Zarathustra and Gandhi.

The next general division is that of Seer, or Prophet. The degrees of measurement are from 51 to 99. There are divisions and subdivisions in this category of Seership. Examples are St. John of the New Testament, Elias of the Old Testament, Jacob Boehme, William Blake, Michelangelo, and thousands upon thousands of others.

The third division is the Helpers. These are from 32 to 50. When a man attains 32 degrees, his psychic body is complete and he is known as a Master. His subsequent incarnations will be those of a Helper. These go to the objective plane in rotation. It is not a particularly welcome experience. Most Helpers lose about 5 degrees in incarnation. Some have been known to lose as many as 15 degrees and had to return to regular cycles of incarnation.

The duty of these Helpers is to work on the spiritual plane and interpret it to men. Some examples are: Francis Bacon, Walt Whitman, Swedenborg, Mary Baker Eddy, Abraham Lincoln, St. Martin—in fact, St. Martin was on the boundary to Seership. Among these are the composers, artists, writers, or any souls whose work raises the vibrations of humans. Some of them are conscious of their identity on the objective plane. If they work with Initiatory Bodies, they have to be.

One must never talk of what one's degree is on the inner planes, if one knows it. Even on the objective plane, in secret fraternal organizations, it is not good to talk of it. If one gets into the habit of not discussing one's own or others' degrees, one will learn the lesson ahead of time, before it becomes really necessary. If a person has a perfectly legitimate reason to inquire about degrees on the objective plane, such as an Officer of an Order, for instance, then one can state what it is.

There is never any need to tell one's degree on the spiritual plane, because an individual himself reveals this to another if his inner eye is opened. It is as simple and easy as it is for us to identify the difference between an Oriental and an Occidental. In other words, it is apparent.

Further knowledge which must be passed on is this. (In fact, all knowledge received must be passed on. We are not to do so indiscriminately—we must not cast pearls before swine—nevertheless the obligation is there.)

Now, there are three types of Initiates. One is a Healer. This can be typified by Mary Baker Eddy, the founder of the Christian Science movement.

Another type is a Teacher. This type is exemplified by Jacob Boehme, Louis Claude de St. Martin, Martin Luther, and many others.

And the third type is a Redeemer. That type is very well exemplified by Gandhi, who is a contemporary historical figure. Invariably, Redeemers meet violent transitions.

Now, the embodiment of all three types in one manifestation or in one body constitutes a living Son of God, typified by Jesus, Buddha, and all Avatars.

Initiates will have all three types of incarnation. We will be Healers, Teachers and Redeemers.

The order of incarnation as to type of initiation is governed by the ray upon which we, as individuals, are. There are seven rays emanating from the Godhead, and each of us is on one of those rays. Our development and expression are governed by the laws of the particular ray whereon we are.

If we have had an incarnation as a Redeemer Initiate and have met a violent end, we will be a Healer or a Teacher next.

These three kinds of Initiate incarnations are symbolized by the three steps leading to an altar, as seen in paintings wherever three steps are shown.

There are seven meanings to the three steps whenever and wherever portrayed mystically, and this meaning of the three kinds of Initiate incarnations is the seventh and highest esoteric meaning.

July 24, 1948

When one enters a truly esoteric Order, one of the first things learned is rules of health, which entail breathing, eating, sleeping and methods of correct thought.

As one progresses, these practices of correct physical living may be done halfheartedly or not at all, and this is detrimental to health. Since one raises one's vibrations spiritually and the body itself becomes less coarse and more sensitive, it is important to follow closely the rules which have been tested for a long time and found best suited to healthy living. That phrase "Know Thyself" is no idle patter. It is a real admonition to each individual to study self and to learn what is best suited to his or her own well-being.

An accumulation of years of improper eating and lack of rest will result in some form of acute suffering which may require hospitalization or an operation.

Another form of disability or the possession of an ailing body is the result of the soul's decision to incapacitate the body to a certain extent so that the physical mind will devote all if not the greater part of its efforts to the problem of reintegration with God.

A very good example of this is Mary Baker Eddy, who founded the Christian Science movement. This movement does great good in teaching correct methods of thought. It is the gateway for many into deeper study of mysticism in the various Initiatory Orders of the world.

One may rest assured that an individual who has learned all the lessons and has attained a high degree of development, as seen by spiritual and not physical standards, will be in perfect health always. This individual knows by experience what to avoid and what to admit into his or her own system, and which practices result in perfect health and which are detrimental to health. Moderation in all things is the best practice.

December 28, 1947

The scattered groups, religions and societies of esoteric nature are slowly merging into one federation. And that is right. One soul starts each movement and each group calls itself by a different name, but their aims and ends are the same. It is only to the undeveloped intellect that another group's methods seem more efficacious. Each has its means to fill the needs of the members it attracts. The heads of these movements know that the movements are all the same.

When the whole federation publishes its list of member organizations, the less progressed souls will see that there is no need to place one above the other and to rush from one to another for the sole purpose of self-aggrandizement.

The only motive for allying oneself with any group is for rendering greater service, with no hope for material reward.

May 13, 1949

The two triangles are symbolical of the gyrating cones of action and interaction which go on between the physical and the spiritual planes. To help men achieve the blending and the balancing of the two, there are seven Initiatory Orders, corresponding to the seven life waves of humanity, which are the seven centers of the universal man.

December 28, 1947

The greatest, most evolved souls seldom hold office in organizations. They direct and influence in the right direction on upper levels of consciousness.

Man advances not by the efforts of any organization but by his own efforts. All that any organization can do is to set forth the laws, and it is up to the individual to apply these laws. Another important function of any organization is to test the individual. Neither the individual nor the organization is willfully directing this function, but matters arrange themselves so that the organization becomes a testing ground for the individual. The individual succeeds or fails, or progresses to another group where he may be of greater service.

The keynote is ever one of service—the best service that one can give to the greatest number.

March 8, 1948

Perhaps the greatest contributor to bringing light into the world was the Salvation Army. A fine organization, but like all organizations it has become too money-conscious.

The Friends are still quietly advancing their barriers against spiritual darkness, but they are not working enough with other people in lectures and broadcasts.

Many organizations think it is enough to feed the spiritual man. The most important function any organization has is to minister at first to the physical man. Once that is done, the individual progresses to work on his soul.

Provision should be made to allow every individual to gain self-respect, and then work toward spiritual Mastership.

After the student has exhausted all that the mundane organizations can give him, he applies to the Initiatory Bodies, whose work is with the Chosen Ones. These teach soul development, cosmic consciousness, and union with the Godhead.

Chapter Nine

▼

Government

January 22, 1948

Many nations pursue a policy of belligerence to control the economic conditions of its neighbors and its own people. This attitude never made for prosperity. Eventually the bellicose one becomes involved in a quarrel with another nation and plunges into misery. The same applies to individuals.

Greatness of soul in the nation, and also in the individual, can be arrived at only through genuine humility. Some day humans will learn this.

Many years ago there was a nation which is no longer in existence. It rose to great power and magnificence, solely through practice of humility. God was with it. Then came aggressive ideas to its leaders, and that destroyed the nation. You call them Atlanteans. Their likeness and achievements have known no parallels since. Seldom, if ever, can a negative aspect persist. If it manifests, it does so only to destroy itself.

Love is the great builder and the only creator for eternity.

March 1, 1948

Many so-called great personalities of history were not really Great Souls, but instruments of forces which used their bodies to gain possession of certain places on Earth. Sometimes the spirit of a country used such methods to drive out an invader or to regain possession of territory or, at times, for aggression. These souls, in subsequent lives, have no recollection of their former glory. They shrug with unbelief and show no interest. Lords of creation ordained it thus.

October-December 1939

It is a fallacy to blame leaders of people for wars, and to exonerate the people themselves. The monomaniacs that are playing power politics are nothing more nor less than individuals who are in tune with the mass emotion of a people and run in front of the destroyers. From Attila, Alexander, Caesar, Napoleon to Hitler and on to today, it is the will of the people and not their leaders that cause bloodshed and destruction.

The terrible thing about it is that they cannot help themselves. They are fulfilling their own laws of being and bringing upon themselves and others the fruits of past causes so that they may learn their lessons in preparing themselves for reintegration with deity.

Cycles of existence that governs governments are actually spirals, with each succeeding round embracing a wider sphere of knowledge, experience and influence. History shows this to be true. Advances in all fields of knowledge show this spiral to greater achievement.

September 7, 1960

There is a great deal of chicanery and underhanded methods being used to gain all kinds of information which may or may not affect national and international policies. This jockeying for power is a fantastic game. Let me turn the pages of events back to recapitulate. America was mixed up with the Spanish Insurrection. God does not want war; man does. The people responsible for fulfilling destinies of nations are the ones under compulsion to act the way they do and effect the policies of nations. Getting a nation to act as a unit is a very difficult thing, and it takes strong personalities to do this. Confusion can be disastrous. Karmic destinies of nations must not affect karmic destinies of individuals adversely if there is no need.

In various nations there are individuals under heaviest karmic conditions. The karmas of these individuals affect their nations more directly than attacks of any other nation in the world.

October 14, 1960

Why does the world tolerate blustering, raving and ranting leaders of nations? Why are such things in the world? Indeed the leaders of humanity are inspired to act the way they do by the hierarchies of their respective nations. When we examine the records of countries we find that there are always karmic obligations of peoples to fulfill, and these determine the makeup of people comprising nations. Your enemy nation now might well be your own nation in the future. Think on that and act accordingly. Each individual prepares his own future every day of his life. Why do individuals live as if they are immune to the consequences of their own actions? They are not evolved enough to realize that their life is continuous, for one; and their religious leaders have not fulfilled their duties to their people by informing them of reincarnation. But more frequently people are born with the remembrance of past incarnations, and that cannot be taken away from any individual. In fact, knowledge of this phenomenon is on the increase all the time.

March 28, 1948

Each country has at least one Master, or there would not be any country. As soon as a particular people have no Master, that nation perishes as a self-governing group.

That is a reason France will never perish. She always has two Masters. Great Britain has only one right now, but will have three before the end of the century. Scotland has none, and that is why she is a part of England. The same is true with Wales. Russia has an embodiment of the Evil Principle, which worships materiality and hurls man further down into devolution.

Germany had this embodiment of the Evil Principle, too. That is why it is no longer a self-governing nation.

America has twelve Masters at the moment. Canada has one. Either this one will go to Britain and there will be two, or Britain will move its government to Canada and there will be two. Those are choices left to the nations.

Therefore, whichever people desire self-government, let them first produce a Master.

September 18, 1948

God allowed Communism to encompass Russia because it was the quickest means for the greatest number of ignorant people to lift their intellects to an ability of dealing with abstract thought. Many minds working in constant conjunction are necessary to make a movement, which is sweeping a large proportion of humanity, work. Communism is the pendulum swinging entirely into matter and denying God.

September 16, 1959

Communism is a demonstration of sheer materiality. It is the lowest sinking of the mind to negation of spirituality. These people are truly asleep in every sense of the word. The system is a mass hypnotism on the astral plane, similar to that of Roman Catholicism up to the Twentieth Century. But Catholicism allows and encourages spiritual development—in fact, the system is based on the premise that man is spiritual and not material. Diametrically opposed is Communism, which says that man is material and not spiritual. Yes, that is the question which arises in all minds—the question is the reason God allows the demonstration of Communism. The truth of the matter is that humanity as a whole is about five thousand years behind in its evolvement. One has but to travel in India, China, or Africa, to get the full impact of this truth. Man as an image of God is truly a debased creature in those countries. It was the same in Russia. Those people inherently do not have the equipment to walk with "one foot in heaven," as it were. They are extremes. When they are mystical, they are totally so. And when they are material, they are totally so. There are only rare cases when these people are "normal." In this light, the people embracing Communism are to be pitied. It will take three generations (sixty years) to erase this scourge from the land where it demonstrates, no matter where it is. Then, there will be a swing in the opposite direction, and a monarchy will be established, an elected monarchy, built on patterns of a Spiritual Hierarchy.

These leaders of Communism have terrible karmas accumulated. Their irresponsible use of power has shed tremendous amounts of innocent blood. This is always a terrible karma. Peaceful coexistence with Communism is not possible. Communism is a total lie. The Communistic mind being what it is, makes the idea impossible. Spiritual evolvement of man is the greatest single force governing mankind, and nothing can stand in its way. Communism imposed itself on those people because they were ignorant. It is a system of thought for the ignorant. "None are so blind as those who will not see," is a true thing, especially so when applied to Communism. All this will pass; only God's will demonstrates, as always.

September 18, 1948

When individuals learn that there is a source from which matter originates and lift their consciousness to delve deeper into the mysteries of manifestation, they will find that their path leads straight to God. They may reluctantly admit an unknown, and inevitably their consciousness rises to the stage where cosmic consciousness bursts upon them and the meaning of God becomes clear. No matter how much or how vehemently truth is denied, it cannot be destroyed because such is the law. And man is ever led to the realization of it, in spite of himself. The compulsion is greater than the resistance of his material mind, because this compulsion arises from that spark within him which is God.

February 27, 1949

God always allows humanity to go on its way, because He wills not to alter the law of creation. The law of creation was amended only once when the Christ power poured forth, and it has not altered since. We can only achieve what the component parts of creation allow us. A combination of elements allows us to achieve new things, but there is nothing absolutely new which comes forth, only a new recombination of things already available. What humanity needs, is a completely new philosophy, which can be caused only by an invention which will alter their lives completely. All enemies of human progress—and there are many such because it is to their advantage to maintain the status quo—are opposed to acceptance of new inventions which alter the manner of human living. They fear, of course, the loss of their own manner of living. And that goes for systems of government and for systems which operate hierarchically. A good example is the rise of new forms of government. The old order resents the brash newcomer, who arrogates all sorts of powers unto itself. But this is the order of things. It cannot be helped, as it will grow and continue.

February 22, 1960

All the people are led to expect a very intelligent leadership. And the leader has to be astute enough to fathom the real will of the people. He has to have enough vision to see the outcome of various decisions. Things are gathering speed and the whole world is accelerating activity. When the changes in government come they will be very gradual, but changing, nevertheless. There will be a greater voice of the people in government. Thus far, it is really factions which are vociferous enough to get their will done. For instance, in your city, it is the real estate people who are running the city and they are doing a very good job, too. But their own interests are served first. That is the picture. And the only reason this is so is because no one else is interested enough to participate in local government. There it is. When people become sufficiently interested in how they are being governed, they will be the governors. Most people blindly follow where they are being led and have no one but themselves to blame when laws are passed which the majority do not like. Things are fantastically simple to understand if one but makes the effort to understand them.

Chapter Ten

Weaknesses

January 26, 1960

Knowing the weakness of humanity, God forgave all who sinned against Him. Humans are so constituted that they are the most inconsistent, unreliable and undependable breed in God's creation. Why? They are mercurial because they have free will, and they do not know themselves why they change their minds. Divine providence always protects them and steers them somehow onto the right paths of spiritual evolvement. They call it luck, but it is really the soul's necessity which does this. Comforting thought.

Pride February 2, 1948

Many years ago there lived an old man who thought he could rule the world. He had the right idea as to the application of laws governing the conduct of men. God gave him a chance and made him ruler of his country. What happened? He lost his humility, plunged his country into needless war, and set his country's well-being back for several centuries.

Such is pride. It is like a thick strong wall between God and man. Laws governing control of pride are simple. When an individual realizes that he has a Christ image inside him, this realization will lift him above any imaginary slights to his personality on the objective plane and teach him humility on the subjective plane.

February 26, 1949

Who can greet the Master? Only those can greet him whose sensitivity makes of them veritable listening posts for the vibrations of the universe. Much venerated is of little value, since many practices have outgrown their value. For example: There is no longer any need for strict forms of diet as a religion. Food should be scientifically evaluated and the individual should eat that which his body requires.

The wearing of habits of special kinds of dress to show a religious mode of life is another valueless practice. Humanity is advancing enough to see the garment which the thoughts of the individual have woven around his body. That is the distinctive garment, of which habits are a symbol. It is no longer necessary to clothe oneself in a distinctive religious habit so that it may set one apart.

Another form of ancient practice which is no longer necessary in view of man's advancement is the practice of abasement in front of individuals of authority. This is nothing but pride. Abasement of flesh before the Christ within is vitally necessary, but abasement before other fleshly forms is ridiculous and stupid. What men need are some sort of guidance, but not to the extent of being an automaton. Men require enough freedom to learn not to transgress nature's laws, and enough to assure spiritual progress.

Greed March 23, 1948

Twice, within human knowledge, has the devastation of world conflagration been unleashed. Mankind will not learn the object lesson of the futility of greed.

Knowledge is becoming harder and harder to acquire. Long years and much suffering are the only way that man learns to develop his soul. Man will learn eventually.

February 18, 1948

Greed for any material possession or condition opens the way to many physical disorders. It will start a train of lies which may hurt others and the individual. The physical payment is usually jaundice. It is so unnecessary to give way to this emotion, because each individual has a goodly supply to draw from on the psychic plane. All he needs to know is to learn how to tap the source of supply. Unfortunately, for some, this requires spiritual development, and most people are lazy.

Self Interest February 28, 1960

Compare life today with what it was in ancient times. We are fortunate to live at present. It has its limitations, too, depending on one's income. And one's income depends on one's earning power and earning capacity. This is very important. Long ages ago, there was ruthlessness in physical life. Today there is ruthlessness on the mental level. Self-interest is still the motivating power behind humanity's manifestation as living beings.

June 27, 1960

Knowledge is a good thing, if one can stand knowledge about some things. Some knowledge is too awful for one to contemplate. Reason would rebel, but that is how the universe runs. All ills of mankind stem from self-interest. This self-interest is at the base of all ills in the world. And there are many ills. Exposure will cure some of them. And some will lose their glamour once they are brought out into the open—things like wars, sex, education, crime, religion, and many others.

Crime March 1, 1960

God saw the wickedness of people of the world—deliberate wickedness that peoples do which you do not dream of in your wildest flight of fancy.

This is the thing which decides what form of universal education man will get to evolve. This sometimes takes the form of want and privation.

Whether people turn to God is a question, too. Sometimes, and quite often, they turn to crime and become even more wicked. It is a puzzle.

Inadequacy October 4, 1959

Inadequacy in people makes them act the way they do. They are aware of their own mistakes and their own shortcomings, so they outwardly manifest surliness or crossness and generally an objectionable mien to forestall others' reactions. Their feeling is that someone else might become aware of what they are really like and manifest displeasure with them. And that is why they cultivate this objectionable mien and make it their armor. This explains the occasional conduct of your near and dear or the ones whom you get to know well. They are, or become aware of, their own shortcomings and do not want others to become aware of them also. At first they are more displeased with themselves than the world. Then they start blaming the world, and that is when they need much love and understanding to help them out of their attitude.

Well-being is wholly a personal attitude. People are unhappy or happy, according to their own personalities. They always blame others for their own faults. Pretty soon they believe that others are responsible for their unhappiness and their condition in life, when it is their own fault. That is the way things are.

Selfishness February 24, 1949

When one wishes well to anyone and opens one's heart to him, one leaves one's defenses open for all sorts of negativities belonging to the other individual to rush in. It is best to have all one's defenses always at work. People are an expression of both good and evil. The more good there is in them, the more spiritual they are; and the worse there is in them, the more material they are.

If people are always effusing over one, there is insincerity usually attached. The effusing one wants to wear down an individual's defenses to establish a pulling process from the defenseless, well-wishing one.

As a whole, people are still a very selfish lot. Some of them are so because of ignorance, and some because of malice. It is necessary to protect oneself always.

March 4, 1948

Fame and fortune are fleeting, yet humanity judges others by that criterion. Rather should humanity be judged by accomplishments. Follow along the dictates of the heart, since it knows all.

Given an opportunity to do good, nine out of ten will not avail themselves of it. Humanity is very selfish. Many an individual has shut the door on his own spiritual development, just by such a lack of charity.

Weak Resolve
March 31, 1948

Weak resolves never discovered the kingdom of God. Follow the dictates of the heart and you will attain it. Many lessons are yet to be learned.

Much help is given which is not apparent. A clear conscience is worth all the gold in the world, and more. It leaves the mind and hearts open to receive instruction. Only the pure in heart attain the kingdom of God.

October 7, 1961

Think of all the people in the world who would like a good smart leader to tell them what to do and when to do it. Their main problem in life is to live. Even the basic rudiments of judgment and evaluations are missing. And never mind decision making. Wrong decisions are arrived at, mostly by happenstance. The main problem of mankind is the hesitation to make a change. Fear of consequences in making changes is the principal reason trouble comes.

Mock Humility
March 13, 1948

Consider those with "belittling themselves" manners. Bring them close to truth if you can. Open their eyes to the possibility of mind development. If left to themselves, their mock humility does a great deal of harm. Humility with full spiritual development is an entirely different thing.

A humility with no spiritual development retards the individual and acts as a pull against spiritual development, also to those around this negative person.

Cowardliness April 4, 1948

When man finds all present favor some measure, he tends to go along with it despite his own convictions, because of his fear to appear different. Pleasure is another factor in deciding how a man will act or react to a given situation. If a man gains pleasure by practices though they are bad for his development, he will nevertheless continue until it becomes a veritable task to break the habit.

It takes courage to stand forth and maintain the right in spite of the majority. The truly great are courageous, when most humanity is cowardly.

Wrong Speech February 28, 1960

Honesty is sometimes a hindrance. It is best to say nothing. Honesty can sometimes destroy the first tender shoots of something wonderful that is coming up for air and struggling for life. Honesty can be brutal and cut it short. It is wise to weigh outcomes of certain things and in a way foretell what the consequence of one's words might be.

March 6, 1948

Speak only of things intended to elevate the individual's life. Do not indulge in idle talk. Listen politely if you must, but do not engage in it.

This is important, as it will enable people to learn of your integrity and wisdom. Your role is ever to teach of the spiritual world. Probably more harm is done in the world by idle chatter than by deliberate malicious talk.

Long ages ago when man's communication of ideas was very simplified, there was little room for misunderstanding the intent. Now the expression of ideas takes form in highly complicated modes of expression, which frequently leads to misunderstanding. Therefore, one who would lead a spiritual life does not talk idly much. Many forms of expression can be simplified too much. Still, one must remain interesting and expound at great length on subjects of universal truth.

The limitation is placed on subject matter rather than volume. To dwell on trivialities is a waste of time, effort, and mental powers. Women most frequently indulge in this form of conversation.

May 19, 1963

Women of the world: Men are more inclined to favor you with a little more ability and brains than before. Indeed, men are considering you more as partners and helpmates. Regard memories of the ages concerning men's treatment of women. They were treated worse than animals, abused more than felons; and if that were not enough, women spoke of men as their lords and masters. This, of course, occasioned all the negative treatment. The situation changes. Women are throwing off the yoke of servitude and showing that they can make their own way in the world without the aid of men. This would not have been possible even fifty years ago.

Chapter Eleven

Current Developments

1940's—1960's December 1942

Nations are being weighed. The righteous in all of them will be blessed, and the evil ones will be destroyed. Especially is the German nation being considered. God will bless the Polish with a mighty nation.

This evil war is allowed because all the people who are not ready for the Son of Man in the new age must perish.

Loved are all the Aolians who will found a new civilization after this war. A large force will crush the Germans in Eastern Europe. All nations will be punished, but one nation will be dissolved from the evil in its heart.

America will be the final victor.

A great force of arms will be directed to sweep over the face of Europe and great will be the devastation when all will be destroyed that was not wrought in the name of the Lord.

Humanity has arrived at the reason for this lesson to be taught. The lesson is significant. Only in His Name will anything endure. Europe will be left a shambles. Marks of the devastation will not be obliterated for a hundred years. Spain will fight again, in spirit if not in deed. It will be too late.

India's population will be torn by internal strife till the rivers run red.

Berlin will be leveled to the ground. All the great cities of Europe will not escape from the wrath of their own sins made real. They destroy themselves. Russia will learn her lesson of trusting in God. Sweden will not be a Judas when she learns her lesson eventually.

Nations brought this war upon themselves by their sins.

Anglia will lose many possessions not rightfully hers. Germany will be divided among her neighbors, the largest part going to Poland. A new order will be formed among the nations of the world. Most of the evil people will be removed and rebirth will bring the innocent into surroundings where it will be unnecessary to sin.

England will be tested to the limit of her capacity to stand pain and humiliation. She will lose India, and Australia will become a free nation like America, independent of Britain. Canada will join the United States as a sister nation, not paying any tribute or being united politically, but relying on each other for protection. God wishes to establish a great sovereign state in Europe, with England at its head for governing purposes, but not levying any duties on the others. Divine Wisdom does not tolerate greed for money or power.

Albania will assume a power over the Adriatic.

Greece will continue being a small peaceful country. Her glories will be reflected in the past. The blond giants who founded her traditions are gone. Only the mixture of the dark Mediterranean is there, incapable of heroic art or literature.

Italy will become the most desirable summering place of Europe, but her political greatness is long past.

All the nations stand in judgment before God. Germany will pay dearly with years of bondage. She will be divided among her neighbors. Poland will arise from the ruins a mighty nation. Hers is the coming civilization of Europe. She will be the crossroads of Europe. But Catholicism, as it is, will no longer stifle her in its bonds. A great new spiritual Catholic religion in a universal sense will be her salvation.

All nations are suffering so that they will be made better. When the snow is on the ground, the Germans will collapse like a huge balloon, never to rise again.

The Armenians are coming up as an erudite nation and will give forth many thinkers.

Russians will be taught that only the works wrought in the Lord's name will endure. Stalin will lead the Russians to victory this winter and then go mad. Stalingrad will not fall. It will be badly burned and people will suffer this winter, but the German army will be annihilated when they are led into a trap. Such obliteration in its totality has never been seen. There will be a mountain of men. Broadly speaking, this will happen very soon. The time as mortals measure it, is very difficult to grasp. So, when a few days are indicated, it may mean weeks, but this is literally a very short time.

Sweden is being a Judas but she will learn her lesson.

Divine aid will be given the Americans with their repulsion of an attempted invasion which will occur in a short time. The whole thing will be a failure from the enemy's side. However, Americans will learn the seriousness of war. The enemy will invade the northern coast of Alaska. They will attempt to strike at the gold fields, but will be beaten.

It is ordained that people should find a means of knowing the extent of evil in men. Only the worthy ones will escape suffering. Great Britain will lose her pride and her humility will be her salvation. America will be the home of wisdom in the world. The East has lost it through degeneration into a complicated system of priest craft. And it is ordained that the New Order should spring in America.

France will have another war. Her halves will unite under fire and sweep the foe from the land. Her ally will be Spain, secretly. France and England will never be foes again. They will help one another to maintain peace in Europe. This will pass within the space of time, when the Selected Brethren decide it should.

God wills that the United States should be a haven and refuge of the White Brethren who rule the world. When Germany is defeated shortly, there will be a surplus of war materials. These must be made into tools to till the soil and feed the worthy.

God will put a great man of an illustrious family on the throne of France when the revolution is at its height.

It is ordained that all the people wishing to be free will be free. The people of the world are coming to a realization that the kingdom of God is within the reach of all. This is their hope, and it is being realized. The people of the United States are the most advanced on this path to self-realization. England and Russia will follow. The Catholic countries will realize that their priest craft has dimmed the shine of truth, which is simple. The cup of gladness is filled for the worthy. Soon it will be time to rejoice. Men of God dwelt among the peoples in ages past and will dwell again. Nations are made dependent on one another for a purpose. In time the Earth's people will be one, and this is one of the first steps of amalgamation. The process is painful. Good things will triumph, for such is the law.

God's love will protect His people from fire and destruction. The downfall of Germany nears. The nation cannot survive its barbarous sins.

March 30, 1943

This war will be fought until each belligerent nation is spent. This war climaxes a series of events which began long ago when the Pope tried to usurp the power of the world. In the final analysis, the Vatican is actually to blame for all this bloodshed. Rome it was that inaugurated the huge paying system which empire countries since then have followed and created the sense of national greed. What Rome did was to follow the pattern set forth by the barbarians she had fought. When a church acquires greed for gold, it ceases being a church and becomes a profit-making enterprise.

December 20, 1942

The Orient will cast off the priest craft that has been shackling it for ages. Great turmoil will result because the religious system is too deeply rooted and it will take a long time to rid the world of it where it is practiced. A terrible and fearful thing is this religion—it is parasitical growth and God will destroy it.

February 22, 1943

The African campaign will last so that Germany's forces will be divided while the European campaign advances steadily. In time to come, Turkey will come into Poland with a Polish army to liberate her. The Germans will fall back into Germany proper. England will close in, also an army from Italy. Fighting will exceed anything up to now. The real fighting will be in Germany.

In the future, the Pope is fleeing to the United States. He knows that Italy will be invaded. The Germans will turn on the Italians and strip them of everything. Even the Vatican will not be spared. In America the Pope will be safest. He is coming incognito. No one will know he is living in New York. At present, such is the state of the Catholic Church because of lack of spirituality to guide itself. It has become an empty shell, but it can be revivified to save itself.

India will be the scene of terrible bloodshed. Gandhi will be dead. England does not belong in India. Her mission there is complete.

March 29, 1943

The Polish people will eventually get a knowledge of better government and compassion to become fit rulers in the world to come. Sheer arrogance, pride and pitiless subjugation of minorities are not virtues to be possessed by the next ruling power. One must be a slave in order to become a master, but one must become a wise master and remember his lessons well so that he will not impose slavery, lest he becomes a slave again to learn anew the lesson which he forgot.

April 6, 1943

God moves in mysterious ways. The whole universe follows one law and comes from one thought wave. The world must lose selfishness and the old races will fuse into transitional lines of evolution. The free people all over the world are choosing their paths now. The chains of enslavement had been forged by each individual separately in his own past. All over the world there are a few Wise Ones in each nation, so that whenever things get too bad they will point out the best to guide the lost ones.

God gave to Poland this enormous cross, but now the days are counted, and the sleeping power of righteousness will arise and conquer unrighteousness. When the Polish army with its standard of a crescent moon enters from the East, then will Poland never again thus suffer and will give a Son of God to further teach humanity.

The Roman faith of the past is no longer needed in Poland. The people have progressed further through suffering and a new era of intelligence is starting. The people must learn truth which was hidden from their understanding. This truth will reign again when the Golden epoch succeeds which will continue two thousand years.

January 2, 1943

God will bestow on the bleeding nation of Poland the greatest honor of all. She will produce the next great Avatar. Watch for him best about 1992.

March 26, 1943

The people of France will arise and fight an invader almost singlehandedly and without arms. In time, France will have the greatest revolution it ever had.

Britain and Turkey signed a treaty where Turkey has rights in the Mediterranean, so that Europeans can go unhindered through her lands.

March 26, 1943

The army of Germany will be utterly destroyed on all fronts so that the Antichrist is exposed to the view. They are sheltering him. The general disintegration will begin next June.

The Japanese army will be beaten.

God wills that Europe become ready for the new cycle of civilization, with brotherly love as the keynote.

July 18, 1943

All nations under Hitler will revolt when the time draws near to invade each one. Hitler and his cohort are the personification of all the evil which the people have built up all over the world—not only the Germans, it must be understood. The reason he manifested in Germany was that they were the ripest to fall under his sway. In every other nation he would have been dismissed as a radical. In Germany, he is being used by a group of five men whose wish it is that Germany rule the world. The only nation which can truly rule the world is the one under which spiritual growth is utterly unhampered. This spiritual growth is the main reason for man to have his being on Earth. The nation whose sole interest is material gain can never rule the world, because it is against the laws of the universe. What can a drop of water do against the might of the ocean? A nation cannot stand against a universe. It will be annihilated. Such is the fate of nations that do not give room for spiritual growth.

April 9, 1943

All events are effects arising from causes. The law of retribution cannot be evaded. The evil unpunished deeds of a lifetime's sojourn will not be punished by any imaginary hellfire; it will be punished right in the flesh on Earth in subsequent lives. We return, again and again to the Earth in one body after another and work toward a goal of spiritual perfection. Turning one's mind toward God brings blessing immediately, and the war did this to the people. The war will be carried into Germany to atone for the terrible sins committed by the Germans. They are guilty of murder and the worst is for them yet to come. The small peoples of all nations have suffered while the big ones waxed fat, but the day of reckoning is come.

December 6, 1942

The United States will win this war because it will be the home of the New Order in the world, which will start in America. We are fortunate that blood will not flow in our land, although Alaska will be invaded.

June 27, 1943

It is ordained that America will be the final victor in this war. The final struggle will be in and near India.

The world must advance in its knowledge at a more rapid pace now, and that is why the whole globe is enveloped in fire. There is an endless stream of souls undergoing birth into surroundings where they will have a better outlook on events and thus see truth.

All nations must unite toward a common goal. So far, they have gathered themselves into two distinct forces. One whose aspirations are strictly tied in with the world of matter, which is impermanent and illusory, will learn that it leads to self-destruction. The other's aspirations, although mainly material, leave room for spiritual growth and development. Since the law of the universe is spiritual, the all-material, or black force, is foreordained to defeat.

December 25, 1942

The pyramid of this civilization is approaching its peak so rapidly that events are happening with rapidity.

March 28, 1943

Good people will not have any suffering in this terrible time.

March 7, 1943

There is famine stalking the world, which will wipe out all but the ones who are ready for the truth. The population will be depleted all over the Earth. As many will be warned as need arises for them to teach the others and make way for the Son of Man.

February 28, 1943

God wills for the whole world to become spiritual. The time is coming when all the people will have the gift of clairvoyance and clairaudience, so it is very important that none use it for selfish purposes. Those not fit for the New Order must have new bodies. That is why the means have been brought about to facilitate the process of this progress. A new race of people is on the way.

April 3, 1943

The ancient Egyptians, come back, will be the first to show the way to Europeans for a world peace. Many wise souls are being born in Europe, after having slept for thousands of years. Now their souls have been entering the cycles of rebirth. They will preach many wonderful truths.

The world is getting ready for the new life. There will always be struggle and pain, but everyone will know what it is all about and struggle effectively toward a spiritual perfection.

God blessed the whole nation of Portugal before the purge of blood it will undergo.

December 13, 1942

Events brought this war about to make way for a new era and another mode of life. Only the Chosen remain to welcome the Son of Man who will teach the philosophy of kindness and love to fellow man.

January 10, 1943

All nations will unite toward a Golden Age, and this war will be the start of bringing them together.

January 8, 1948

Live, all you people at peace with one another, for you do not harm anyone but yourselves. Many Great Souls are working these days to maintain the peace on Earth which is sorely needed by mankind. Greed is the only motive which impels men to deeds of violence. This greed takes many forms, all of them detrimental to human growth and development.

January 4, 1948

Many leaders of humanity today are in touch with the Cosmic Intelligence which is ruling the world. They are consciously the instruments of God's will in the affairs of men. They have received due preparation and are fulfilling their destinies. Their roles may be minor but their influence is far-reaching.

Glories incomprehensible to man are their reward for working the Will of God.

Great Souls, incarnated and not, have pitted their strength to counterbalance the forces which are pulling the Earth to the next lower sphere of vibration. They have saved the world, but may not be able to prevent a cataclysm. The souls who are necessary to the advancement of civilization will be removed from the scene of danger. Those who lose their bodies inadvertently will be given new bodies almost immediately.

These are the times of the New Dispensation. And these are the times of the great choosing, whether souls will advance to the highest development afforded by the Earth conditions, or whether they will wait for a new Earth chain. Souls are given a chance to change bodies out of their birth cycle to live in environments which will give them proper opportunities for advancement.

January 5, 1948

As it is, the Earth's inhabitants are making wonderful progress in spite of their being about five thousand years behind in evolution, and this through their own fault. They are being helped by the deluge of Great Souls which have come on Earth to lift its vibrations so it will not perish.

Still this influx of higher vibrations cannot stop the cataclysm which will alter the land surface of the world. That land near Europe which is mostly coveted by greedy nations will be destroyed. The greed, itself, will destroy it. Poor humanity. Some day it will learn, but always the hard way.

January 14, 1948

Long ages ago, man could afford to be slow of perception and development. But now, since the vibrations of the world have been raised, he has to come right along with it or be left behind for countless millions of years.

Conditions force man to raise his vibrations into a higher sphere of activity.

Plants are adapting themselves to the new order of things, too. New varieties and mutations are occurring continually.

February 2, 1948

Glad tidings flow to mankind continually on wings of celestial messengers. They flow over all and benefit all in some way. These are rays of very high vibrations. A new force is beginning to work its way into this constellation.

In a few months the effects of these rays will begin to tell upon humanity. Acts of unselfishness will be commonplace. From seldom known sources, words of wisdom will come to help humanity. The Hierarchy is altering leadership, you must understand. Follow these changes and you will notice pronounced changes in various religious movements on the Earth plane. Fellowship and brotherhood will be emphasized.

February 10, 1948

God brings enlightenment when a necessary condition prevails which seems to cause much suffering among men. The enlightenment explains the necessity of the condition—what brought it into being, and the results. Such a condition prevails now in the world. It is necessary to break the power of the false leaders who are enslaving souls which rightfully belong to God's harvest. The time will come when all will turn to the only God who brings salvation. Humanity must turn to the One God, and not to any ideas and ideals established only for material gain. God allows these works of the false prophets to exist so that their empty results can be experienced and to show that they cannot prevent souls from progressing to a higher state of consciousness.

February 25, 1948

Lo, the day draws near when God's armies will inundate the Earth and throw protecting cordons around His Chosen Ones. The rest who did not choose to work in righteousness will be left to their own workings of the effects caused by their evil actions.

April 26, 1948

There is now a necessity of change upon Earth as far as human conduct is concerned. All destructive agents have been isolated and distributed over the surface of the Earth where they will be of least effect. The majority of humanity will be subjected to a series of vibratory forces which will prepare them for a better scheme of living. All those not ready to go with the new plan of life will be withheld from incarnating until a later scheme of a world system, because those souls would only hold back the spiritual development of the rest of the human family. Their ray will be changed and they will no longer be able to contact the Earth because of its raised vibrations.

In this scheme, only those who are ready for spiritual sight, hearing and perception will comprise the human family.

February 16, 1949

Be it ever so small, every event has some significance. For instance, the weather has been arranged in the world because of work against war. One force is working toward horrors of war and a strong force is working toward peace. The upset in uniformity of weather has stopped scheduled operations for further bloodshed in the world. The only serious casualties have been the freezing of animals which were destined for the horrors of slaughter houses, anyway. This was a comparatively painless release.

Aggravation is never excusable; and differing ideologies bring enlightenment to those in need of them.

August 23, 1950

The conflagration starting to erupt in Asia is the beginning of a worldwide upheaval and much destruction. The Forces of Right and Left are locked in a struggle to achieve supremacy either by one side or another. By violence will the force of darkness be overthrown.

Although it looks like a senseless loss of life and unnecessary bloodshed, only those who are supposed to survive will do so. The time of the great choosing has arrived. Either to go forward toward conscious reintegration with God or make another start in another earth period. That is also why there is a sudden outburst here and there among religious bodies. These outbursts of religious feeling serve their purpose, too. Some are narrowly bigoted; nevertheless, they are the means by which a group of souls makes an audible, conscious, physical assertion of their intentions to serve God. Not one soul in the world will be missed. All will have their turn. The reason hostilities ceased for a while was to give those souls who had lost bodies accidentally, to be born anew in order to make their choice.

May 5, 1955

Evolved personalities in groups can generate fantastically tremendous power. The power of thought with singleness of purpose is used to achieve a result. This is important at this time, because the whole world is on the brink of disaster and utter destruction of civilization.

January 24, 1960

Henceforward people will be more spiritually aware. Their efforts will be toward a better life, with greater understanding of other people's problems. Of course, no one can really understand what is affecting another person's well-being, but at least the effort will be made to help others solve their problems.

Mankind up to the Twentieth Century has been extremely selfish, caring only for its own needs, and there is reason for that. The outlook has to be selfish when growth is going on. But with the Aquarian age the signature is Outpouring, and this will extend to individuals. The only way this will happen is when a wave of compassion will pass over humanity, inspiring each to like endeavor. The particular vibrations of the Aquarian age do this. The age will create an earnestness in individuals which will be directed to others and also self. It will be a joint interest—self and others.

July 4, 1960

The Lord God of our Earth has decided to bring forth a new type of man, one capable of great achievements. This man will dominate all kingdoms and all kingdoms will yield their secrets unto him. Long ages are behind man and he took aeons to climb out of the primeval ooze, but the climb has been steady if somewhat slow. Mind is coming into alignment with all other bodies and man is reaching that perfection for which he was destined from the beginning. When all creatures walk in amity on the face of the Earth, then God's will is fulfilled.

July 24, 1960

A stupendous thing has happened to humanity. It has reacted favorably to a series of incantations sounded forth by the Masters of Being who dwell eternally on this Earth. Also, a Hidden One, not usually taking notice of affairs dealing with humanity because it lies away from his province, which is away and beyond mere humanity, took this exceptional notice and lent his interest if not active participation in the goings on, and such was the unprecedented effect of his vibration that man's progress spurted forth immeasurably. All over the Earth, every human being has felt a quickening of mind, body, and spirit.

September 15, 1961

Consider the world situation today. A major catastrophic war can be unleashed on humanity which will almost wipe out the human race. This state of affairs was inevitable, though. The atomic weapons would have been discovered, one way or another.

September 12, 1961

America and Russia are locked in a great struggle. America has the edge, however. All is going forward toward a good solution. The Golden Age's arrival depends upon all the dark forces' annihilation, and this is being accomplished. The wicked all must go. This is indeed a time of reckoning.

November 14, 1961

The world is in a sorry state, and only because of the personal ambition of a few men.

Russia is doomed to fall and its leaders know this. You cannot enslave a people for long. Also, you cannot stay in a Godless state for too long. The leaders suffer, too.

Turkey is the key to Europe's salvation and the breaking of bondage. Turkey has a key role to play on the stage of world affairs. She will have an inspired leader who will make the right moves. He will be guided divinely. When people need help and they ask for it, they will receive it.

The Present February 16, 1968

The Negro problem in America goes back to the Thirteenth Century, when the Great Ones sat in conclave and planned the opening of the American continents to occupation by the people of Europe.

It takes from two to three hundred years for any plans to percolate down to the physical plane for action when it involves mass movements of peoples. And it took about that long between the voyaging of the Norseman and the Mediterranean navigators to establish the existence of a land beyond the Western seas.

The respective race spirits, who belong to a particular level in the angelic hierarchy, attended the conclave regarding the American continents. And the causes for having this conclave convene were the plight of the two Indian race spirits in America. The lesser evil confronting one of the Indian race spirits was his inability to raise his people higher than a certain level of the astral plane which constituted their heaven. This Happy Hunting Ground afforded no advancement of consciousness between incarnations. The people could not raise their consciousness into the higher mental levels necessary for their advancement. Ingredients were missing supplying the stimulus of planting a germ which would evolve into a mind capable of abstract thought.

By far, the greatest evil was an astral embodiment of fearsome aspect suffused with serpent power, which was an object of worship by the people of the other Indian race spirit. Terrible rites were performed and blood flowed freely to appease the insatiable appetite of this astral Thing.

These two Indian race spirits asked for help. The law of reciprocity has to be observed; and in order to receive, one must give.

The first race spirit brought a cornucopia of foods that was not available on other continents. The second one brought gold.

Race spirits of all peoples were in conclave. The needs of the American continents' peoples were stated. The other race spirits deliberated on their own people's capabilities for supplying the needs of the America's peoples.

The first Indian race spirit's people needed the addition of Caucasian blood. The second race spirit needed people infused with Christ power to burn up the astral demon and to lead his people onto the Christ path for evolvement.

The race spirits of Britain and France stepped forward to aid the first Indian race spirit and took the cornucopia of food to divide between them.

The race spirit of Spain stepped forward to aid the second race spirit and took the skins filled with lumps of gold. The lumps were actually five-sided and each side had the shape of a pentagon. The race spirit of the Bear people (Russians, you understand), stepped forward too, to offer aid to the second Indian but was told to prepare Christ-infused people in his own land. However, should Spain fail, the Indians of the second Indian race spirit would incarnate in Russian lands. The Russians and the Indians of the second Indian race spirit emanated from a point in Asia. The Eskimos also belong to this emanation.

About this time, the Negro race spirit stepped forth to state his problem. His people were the least evolved of all but had the capability of the fastest evolution of any peoples, given the right set of circumstances. His payment was the most precious of all. He offered the manpower services of his people and slowly put on the chains of slavery for five hundred years. This was stupendous and unprecedented. Never before had a race spirit himself donned the chains of slavery for a period of time.

Six race spirits stepped forth and picked up a length of chain hanging from the Negro race spirit. They made vows agreeing to retribution for abuse of Negroes to be immediate, swift, and in kind. The "in kind" aspect entails incarnation in a Negro body, immediately, of those who abuse the people of the Negro race spirit.

This explains the situation currently on the American continent.

February 17, 1968

Why could not each race spirit work out the problem with his own people? It must be understood that each race spirit is a member of the angelic hierarchy. This kingdom is evolving even as that of the humans. The race spirit, however, knows the lacks and needs of his people. Should the needs of his people involve the properties of the peoples of another race spirit, He must ask for them and give payment.

The angelic hierarchy evolves through service and cooperation with each other. Since the human kingdom was created to become higher than the angelic kingdom, the angels are in effect preparing their own Masters whom they will serve. There is never any ruling on their part over the human kingdom. Their role is ever one of service. Since they lack the earth element in their being, they can never experience suffering. They can express joyousness of varying intensity.

Therefore, the results of that conclave of race spirits, under the guidance of the Great Ones of the solar system, are manifesting on Earth today.

On the whole, the working of their plan was successful. There were unexpected peaks of activity running counter to the general flow of action, but these were overcome, leveled out and redirected.

The Spanish peoples made several mistakes. They were overcome by the power of gold and appropriated more than they had been allotted by the second Indian race spirit. The gold has now been transferred to the people of the Bear and the Indians are incarnating in the Asian part of Russia. The Russians must supply the Christ consciousness in manifestation for the evolvement of its people. Great and terrible are the fate of those who resist the manifestation of God's laws.

Another Spanish mistake was the imposition of their discipline on the Indians of the first Indian race spirit. These Indians had moved en masse to the borders of the second type of Indians, and the Spanish tried to impose their type of civilization and discipline on them without any great success.

Still another Spanish mistake was the enslavement of the Indians, since their race spirit had not put on chains.

The mistakes of the Spanish were occasioned by their enthrallment with the Taurean age vibrations. As long as the bull ring continues to be the source of their greatest worship, that is how long they will continue being poor in every conceivable aspect of being. A pity. They have the ingredients for being a great and mighty nation—in fact, an example for other peoples.

The failure of the Spanish opened the way for the peoples of the British and French race spirits to flow Westward. The people of the British race spirit succumbed to the power of gold they were not entitled to, and they have financial troubles to this day. They are even off the gold standard. As long as they covet the gold of the Indians that is how long they will have financial problems. The gold in the Americas must be used only for the benefit of its native peoples—the Indians. The British race spirit's people, and all the people who have joined them, are only entitled to a tenth of the gold. The other nine-tenths must be used for the welfare of the Indians.

On the Christ consciousness aspect, there was success by all the cooperating peoples.

The Spaniards mingled their blood with that of the Indians to supply them with the necessary type of corpuscles vibrating in cruciform aspect. Also, the people of the other European nations did similarly. Vehicles were prepared and are being prepared to this day, as fit for manifesting the Christ consciousness. Nothing can stop this process, no ideology, no philosophy, no political imposition of restrictions. It is in the blood and will manifest itself.

As for the Negro race, their race spirit rose up after kneeling bowed for five hundred years and stretched out his hands and feet and the chains dropped off. The peoples enamored of their use of the Negro peoples' free service sought to impose slavery on them again, but without success. Bloodshed and suffering resulting from war were futile.

Much emotion generated through the abuse of the Negro people created its own results.

The abusers were incarnated into Negro bodies and are the agitators of today who are chafing under the restrictions they themselves had created. The abused Negroes, who had been overcome by emotions of hatred and vengeance, were and are being reborn as white people. They are the ones who don white robes with hoods and burn crosses and generally terrorize their former abusers who are now in Negro bodies.

The true Negroes who have evolved in the short span of five hundred years are today the legislators, professionals, and artists. Their phenomenal advance in the five hundred years surpasses the rate of evolvement of any other race on the face of the Earth.

The hatreds of the abusers reborn in Negro bodies and the Negroes reborn in Caucasian type bodies will take two more generations to burn out and for the balance to be established. The arrogance on one part and the viciousness on the other part—pitted against each other—will consume each other.

The Jewish religion affords seven incarnations to lift the consciousness to the solar plexus. Also, some esoteric Orders of the hexagram type tiling ritual affords the same opportunity of raising consciousness from the sacral to the solar plexus center.

Progressing from that to the Way of Christ is but a step through the waters of baptism. Some Negroes have gone through the baptism by virtue of forgiving their abusers and have bypassed the Jewish faith. Truly their faculty for rapid advancement into Christ consciousness is phenomenal.

June 1, 1957

The Negro race, almost exclusively polarized in the sacral center physically, is gradually amalgamated into the Jewish race. The Hebrew religion is their normal step forward. This is an advancement. The Jews, psychically, are for the most part polarized in the solar plexus. They inherited this from the Egyptians. The ancient Egyptians failed in their mission, and their monotheism was transferred to the Hebrews.

It takes a long time for religions to die out. When they are no longer needed to fill a people's requirements, they go out of existence. For instance, the religion of the Taurean age still has vestiges existing. It reached its peak of high effectiveness in Mithraic rites. The highlight was the sacrifice of the bull.

It is this ancient memory of man which accounts for the cowboy craze. Also, there is bull fighting still flourishing in Latin countries. The bullfighter, in a sense, is the priest officiating in the bullring by despatching the bull after his own display of skill in performing the ritual of baiting the bull into rage before the sacrifice, when the bull is slain.

The cowboy, in a sense, enacts the same role when he rides herd, ropes, brands and forwards the cattle eventually to the ultimate sacrifice in a slaughter house. There is a real cowboy cult finding expression in rodeos, where the skills inherent to this calling are exhibited. Interestingly, both the bullfighter and the cowboy wear distinctive costumes to set them apart.

It is an interesting thing to view and to consider the backwash of a religion, long gone, yet surviving as a cult of some sort in the social scheme of things.

The cowboy cult is kept going through drama, as seen on the motion picture screen or on television. The interesting aspect of the cowboy cult is that the cows, bulls, calves, heifers—in short, the animals themselves, are not of prime importance anymore. There is always a conflict of good and evil. But blood still flows, pictorially if not factually. The elements of good and evil, the blood theme, and the triumph of good are all there.

The American Indian going into the Mormon faith is still in the Taurean age, but their animal is the buffalo. However, the buffalo symbolizes the bull of the Taurean age. The theme of the symbolism finds one link in Mormonism by use of the ox (Taurean symbol, also) in the baptismal font.

At first, the bull was the god Apis in Egypt, to whom humans were sacrificed. With the passing of the Taurean age the bull became the sacrifice, and this was the theme of the Mithraic rites.

To this day, the bull is still being sacrificed in some countries in the name of sport. The cowboy cult carries the theme, but in dramatic form where it concerns itself with the ethical aspects of life.

June 1, 1957

The Mormon religion's original intent was to use the bull theme with the American Indians, but the race spirit (archangel) could not lift them much above the astral plane of consciousness. It was decided to merge the Indian race with the White race. Hence the terrible slaughter of Indians by the White race, so that the Indians would be immediately reborn into the White race. Each Indian killed by a white individual got a white body and went into the Mormon religion. Now this pertains to the Indians whose source is Atlantis. It does not pertain to the Indians whose source is a point in Asia. The Asian ones go into Catholicism. From the finding of the tablets by Smith to 2500 A.D. is the period of the changeover. By 2500 A.D. there will be no more full-blooded Indians left in America.

Joseph Smith, a White Brother, took incarnation to bring the tablets to light. He accomplished his mission and chose martyrdom, not wishing to undergo the hardships of pioneering, since it was not a karmic obligation on his part. It was the same with his brother. Both are now working on the higher astral plane, bringing Indian souls into incarnation into the White race.

The greater majority of these Indians are not evolved enough to go into the "pure" White race and are coming into mixtures where the white strain is diluted. A "pure" white individual has a cross of light in each blood corpuscle.

The Future June 3, 1963

Now all the people in the world have been measured and have made their decisions regarding soul progress. In the very near future great changes will occur. We, the Teachers, have a great work to do with humanity.

July 11, 1943

All great nations must become highly spiritual. The iron age is passing, as indicated by the increasing use of substitutes for iron. The time will come when all use of iron will be stopped, because better materials will have been found. When the age of iron passes, the golden age begins, and then truly good living becomes a fact instead of remaining a dream.

January 3, 1943

The status of women will be elevated, because in the golden age women will rule on an equal footing with men.

August 11, 1961

The future of man is very glorious on Earth. The forces of good and righteousness will prevail, and that will make it necessary for the opposition to take itself off or to perish.

March 13, 1960

God prepares a glorious future for man if he passes the tests set for him. Man on Earth is not the only man in creation.

September 18, 1959

There are other inhabited worlds, but the mankind on them is vastly different from that on Earth. For instance, there are plant people on one planet. This is difficult to conceive, but aeons have bred plants that have reached this extremely high point of evolvement.

Human life on Earth is a terrifically unique kind of intelligence. There are not many planets that have evolved beings like ours. Some beings on other planets would frighten us very much, even as we would frighten them. We are not the most highly evolved, though. There are humans on other planets whose evolvement surpasses ours above and beyond our wildest conception. They have fully evolved ethereal, or ghost bodies, which they can shape into any image they want and send them out into the universe on exploration missions. That is the fashion in which many, many of them have kept track of human evolvement on this planet from time immemorial. This sounds strange, but it is really a very simple process.

March 13, 1960

There are men on other planets. These have passed tests and have had avenues of development opened to them that would stagger the imagination of man on Earth. These men on other planets do not need vehicles to travel. They can project their consciousness at will. Things which are a deep and mysterious secret to man here on Earth are an open and used method on other planets. Man can look like a plant or a fish or a weird creation, but the high level of evolvement can still make him a man. Think of things accomplished by man, and realization will come that actually he did not accomplish such a great deal. Things that men have made are marvelous, but in essence they amount to very little. The most important thing is how much man has evolved inwardly. How much has his mind grown to live in wisdom and godliness. Think of how man has slaughtered his own kind through the ages, how cruel he has been to his own kind and to lesser kingdoms in nature; and then how he has cheated, stolen, and thwarted progress; and you will realize how important it is to prevent more power from being given mankind before it is ready to use it for the betterment of creation. Things are not the way they appear on the surface. They have hidden meanings, too. It is for man to sharpen his faculties and learn to discern reality wherever it is.

January 1, 1961

When man will have achieved clairvoyance—and that will be an accomplished fact in the not too distant future—then his progress will be more rapid because he will be able to see things more clearly, of which he sees now only the outside, and only the side presented to his vision, at that. "Look lively," is an expression that will have a great deal of meaning. In fact, the expression could be altered to "Hear lively," and so on with all the other senses. In this way man will have the ability to regard any object and/or person and will instantly know everything that there is to know about the object or person. This is a long way off yet, but it is coming.

August 20, 1960

The time is coming when a human being's development will enable him to roam time at will, backward and forward. A human being will be able to read others' minds at will, or will be able to communicate thoughts without uttering a sound. Conscious projection of self into any age, past, present, or future, will be a matter of will. This is not a pipe dream; this is a verity in existence now. The idea staggers the imagination. Nevertheless, it is absolutely true.

June 20, 1960

The Aquarian age is one of the greatest significance and great strides in the scientific sense will be made. Men will communicate with intelligences which are as far beyond the human understanding as man is above the animal consciousness.

Consider the various plant kingdom manifestations. These are as varied as the fishes in the sea. Yet plants have a sensory life and a feeling. They respond to influences in nature. They react to stimuli. It is a curious kind of response based upon the immediate requirement of sustenance and growth of the plant. Yet this very elementary, sensory life manifestation is capable of a high degree of evolvement and demonstration of a unique kind of intelligence which would fascinate a human being.

An approach to comprehending this kind of intelligence can be had from a study of psychology, especially that aspect which considers physical reactions to external stimuli. This sensory type of investigation is only a preview of the depths to which men will understand the evolvement of the plant kingdom in the future. This is slated to happen.

When Christ pours forth upon the Earth, a concentrated amount of His power, all kingdoms in creation must respond. This Second Coming of Christ will affect the plant kingdom terrifically. Man feeds upon lower kingdoms, and this aspect of plant response is needed.

July 19, 1948

God brings love into lives of individuals so that they will learn the meaning of that greater love which envelops the universe. Long ages ago, man was incapable of that earthly love which is commonplace now. In the future greater love will be commonplace and earthly love will be an elementary emotion.

Full realization comes only from an intense application of self to problems at hand and meditation upon them.

September 4, 1953

A new religion will sweep through Europe, a religion which will start in the Balkans. It is a sort of Muhammadanism, but not the kind we know today. It is of a more spiritual and esoteric character, more like Sufism, which is Muhammadan esotericism. This religion will take over all of the Russian territory and sweep Westward through the European continent. The process will take about five hundred years. All this will result from a Russian defeat, when the whole nation will turn to God because everything else will be lost.

In the eyes of the Masters of humanity, all religions are one; merely different aspects of the same truth are presented. To Them it makes no difference what religion is practiced as long as it achieves the purpose of reintegrating humanity with God. And after the Left is subjugated in Russia, the beaten Russians will get a new religion.

August 5, 1961

Wars are the only evil persisting, and this is not man's fault. He is not to blame for wars. There is an evil outside himself which makes wars. Mankind is conducting its own private war against wars, but even collectively it is not strong enough to overcome them. When a common danger looms confronting all of humanity, then it will present a united front and dispel wars forever. Indeed, this time is not too long in coming. Long ages ago, mankind was at the mercy of the animal kingdom and of the elements, much more so than at present. But now the picture is gradually changing.

January 6, 1948

Many impulses sent forth from the spiritual plane are yet to be discovered and brought into objectivity. Marvelous things are to come, like individual swift transport to all parts of the globe.

Control of seasons is coming, which will give full summer and even temperatures to the globe. The release of frozen wastes will inundate the northern part of Europe and Asia, leaving only the mountain tops as islands.

All food will be centrally prepared and dispensed through an intricate system of pneumatic tubes all over cities. This will eliminate waste.

These are only a few things which already are in their idea stage, awaiting sufficiently developed souls to attain attunement with them and bring them into being on the material plane.

Photography may seem wonderful, but a more wonderful refinement of that art will be the photographing of thoughts as they radiate from an individual's head.

July 5, 1960

God ordained that surface-of-the-Earth travel be the most efficient that man can devise. Space travel is an outgrowth of man's own intelligence.

August 13, 1961

Rightly, man should not have a physical body. That was his mistake. He should have his astral body as his lowest and most dense vehicle of expression.

In his astral body man was truly free. The lower man sinks into matter, the less freedom he has. In fact, this going out into space will give him still less freedom. He is trying to find another habitat with less people. He will find conditions less conducive to freedom outside.

August 11, 1961

Bringing life to other planets may be in the scheme of things, but they are not for the good of man. Each planet is peopled with its own kind, and communication is possible if one has the necessary inner evolution. Think how exciting it would be if humanity as a whole was learning to extend its consciousness out into the universe instead of fussing around with physical means to get itself off into space.

July 10, 1961

When God created the world, He made the heavens and everything in them. He also made all kinds of conditions on these other planets. Life on these planets would impose extreme limits on man, as far as environment, food, and atmosphere is concerned. Man, establishing colonies on other planets, would be faced with the same conditions that he is faced with on Earth, but multiplied because he is not built for conditions prevailing there. Let us imagine that an actual colony was established on Mars. Its extreme lack of oxygen would make it imperative for man to manufacture large qualities to fill his needs. The same goes for everything else. Each planet has its own conditions, and none of them duplicate those found on Earth.

Invasion of other planets is on the way, too. Many individuals, souls if you will, already have this power and ability but cannot make it known, because it would not be safe to communicate their knowledge to the "animals" who walk in the guise of men. It is true that each individual has animal-like characteristics, and these will have to be eliminated before man can become human.

June 8, 1963

Consider the moon. Men will reach it. Men will know much about other worlds, but so little about themselves.

January 3, 1948

Great Souls may find an altogether propitious time to demonstrate a law which will become visible to humanity. Fit individuals are inspired to build or put forth said manifestation, and humanity hails a new discovery.

Interplanetary communication is the next great discovery. The initiatory step is even now taking place, but the greatest strides are being made on the other planet. This event will weld the Earth into one unity. Humanity's one great uniter is fear of a common foe. And the time has come for humanity to start working together for a common advancement. The Great Souls have decided to introduce this so-called menace to civilization to bring them out of their childish wrangling. Of course, this experience will be beneficial to the denizens of their respective planets. You have no name for this planet because you cannot see it. Mathematicians can guess its orbit because of unexplainable variations in Earth's orbit. Of course, it blots out the part of the sky where we could see it if it reflected light. Individuals having ability to project themselves have seen it. Records of esoteric groups have information of this planet but they guard it closely. The residents of this other planet are far more advanced than you because, although they are corporeal, they are not learning the lesson of duality.

This will be the first time in creation that the great experiment of corporeal visiting of other planets will be tried. Men's minds have been prepared for this these past few decades.

And the results are as eagerly awaited by the Lord of Creation as by the Great Souls.

March 12, 1960

Things are really looking up for interplanetary travel, and astronauts will not find it too difficult to carry on the work started in this century.

May 22, 1960

When the time comes for humanity to see the new world, it will give off a dim red glow. That is the reason some planets behave erratically, unexplainably enough, in particular places of their orbit, because they react to the presence of the body which is in their vicinity. Our instruments are not delicate enough to plot its course. Now and then vague splotches and forms have appeared in photograph plates, which are very sensitive, but astronomers are at a loss to explain the phenomena. This new planet is forming between the orbits of Venus and Earth, and it will receive the outcasts of humanity from this Earth, when the decisions are all made. Now is the time of choosing. Either forward toward reintegration with God, or back to another round of material existence until the lessons of life are learned. Of course, there are all the animals who have achieved individuality, and they will come in as people on the next Earth. This Earth will become a moon for the next Earth. There was a time, incidentally, when this Earth had two moons, but one of them has since disintegrated.

March 12, 1960

There is great danger looming for mankind from outer space. This is not talked about but is known to only about a score of people in the world. The planet, or celestial tramp, had missed the Earth, but it may not miss the second time because of the spiral motion.

April 11, 1943

God oversees the progress of the world. The time will come when empires will vanish, but it will be after a huge cataclysm which will happen on the Earth which will alter the face of the Earth and its climate. Such a cataclysm will be anticipated by ones who know and they will migrate to a section of the world high up in the clouds. These people will be of the last race and will be of such huge numbers that they will be strong enough to found a vast nation based on brotherly love and it will govern the whole world.

January 4, 1943

The creation of intelligences of superior quality will guide men to their ultimate destination. In time, man will be a superior intelligence and will guide other men on other planets.

INDEX

Absorption, 54
African, 163
Air, 40, 157
Alaska, 161, 165
Albania, 160
Alexander, 147
Amenhotep IV, 15
America, 102, 147, 149, 159-161, 163, 165, 172-173, 178
Andrew, 102
Andromeda, 16
Angels, 59-61, 84, 131, 174
Animal Kingdom, 4-5, 7, 9, 41, 60, 72, 183
Animals, 5-6, 8-10, 27, 38, 53, 65-66, 72, 82, 88, 98, 118, 158, 170, 178, 184, 186
Annunciation, 23
Antichrist, 164
Aolians, 159
Aquarian Age, 22, 171, 181
Aquarius, 112
Art, 59, 90, 104-105, 108-109, 121, 160, 183
Asia, 170, 174, 178, 183
Astral, 7, 13, 25, 29-30, 77, 103-104, 112, 117, 149, 173, 178-179, 183-184
Astrology, 109
Atlanteans, 98, 146

Atlantis, 119, 178
Attila, 147
Australia, 160
Avatars, 21, 142

Bacon, 141
Baptism, 16, 21, 24, 177
Beliefs, 63
Bethlehem, 26
Bible, 20, 31-32, 35-37, 62-63, 94, 107
Blake, 141
Blood, 28, 51, 72, 98, 150, 165, 167, 173, 176, 178-179
Boehme, 141-142
Brahma, 140
Buddha, 45, 140, 142
Buddhism, 24
Buddhists, 20

Caesar, 147
Canada, 149, 160
Cataclysm, 167-168, 186
Catholic, 17, 71, 107, 161-163
Catholicism, 149, 160, 178
Centers, 14-15, 43, 67, 70, 81, 114, 124, 144
Ceylon, 33
Chord, 3, 93
Chosen People, 112
Christ, 7, 12-13, 15-22, 24, 27-30, 36, 40, 49, 55-56, 58, 71, 73, 105, 107, 110, 124, 150, 153, 173, 175-177, 182
Christian Science, 36, 142-143
Christianity, 14, 20, 23-24, 30, 35, 40, 133
Churchianity, 51

Civilization, 87, 98, 113, 128, 159-160, 164, 166-167, 170, 175, 185
Clairvoyance, 69, 166, 181
Classics, 104
Color, 5, 77, 93, 113, 124
Commandments, 42, 45, 51-53, 89
Communism, 149-150
Concentration, 54, 57, 121
Conduct, 42, 62, 111, 123, 152, 155, 169
Conscience, 43, 156
Consciousness, 2, 4, 8, 12, 14, 20, 23-24, 27-28, 41-42, 44-45, 47-48, 50, 59, 63, 68-70, 72-73, 81, 83, 85, 89, 92, 94, 110, 118, 121, 123, 132-133, 144-145, 150, 169, 173, 175-178, 180-181, 184
Constellation, 66, 168
Creation, 3, 6-8, 12-13, 19, 22, 53, 55, 68-70, 77, 82, 85, 97-99, 103, 113, 118, 121, 123, 126, 139, 147, 150, 152, 179-182, 185-186
Cross, 13, 16, 21, 23, 35, 74, 164, 179
Crown, 114
Cycle, 64, 74, 79, 84, 98-99, 123, 127, 164, 168
Cycles, 42, 141, 147, 166

Decalogue, 60, 113, 135
Defenses, 155-156
Destiny, 49, 59, 81-84, 124
Diamonds, 4
Disciples, 30-33, 35-39, 98, 111, 125
Discipleship, 120, 125-126
Divorce, 78
Dream, 95, 116, 154, 179, 181
Duality, 4, 74-78, 97, 185
Earth, 2-3, 6-24, 28, 38, 42, 44, 47, 52-53, 56, 59-60, 66, 72, 74-81, 84, 86, 92-94, 97, 101,

106, 110-112, 116-119, 126, 128, 131, 134, 147, 162, 165-172, 175-176, 179-180, 182, 184-186
Eddy, 141-143
Edison, 88
Education, 60, 85, 90, 103, 154-155
Egypt, 33, 119, 178
Egyptians, 14, 35, 46, 60, 166, 177
Eightfold Path, 45
Einstein, 88
Element, 4, 40, 60, 71-72, 78, 98, 175
Elemental, 106
Elementals, 79, 106
Elias, 141
Elohim, 112
Emotions, 14, 60, 81, 134, 138, 176
England, 102, 148, 160-163
Essenes, 24-26
Ethics, 123
Europe, 119, 159-161, 164, 166, 168, 172, 182-183
Events, 84, 86, 119, 127, 147, 162, 165-167
Evolvement, 4, 8, 10, 12, 17-20, 23-24, 27, 49, 66, 68, 71, 82, 88-89, 91, 108, 123, 125-127, 129, 134, 149-150, 152, 173-176, 180-182, 184

Fall, 6, 8-9, 63, 161, 163, 165, 172
Fate, 2, 82-83, 165, 175
Fates, 112
Father, 24, 62
Fear, 29, 39, 45, 51, 102, 113, 128, 137, 151, 156-157, 185
Fire, 2-3, 5, 66, 71-72, 79, 118, 161-162, 165
First, 2, 8, 21, 28, 31-32, 44-45, 50, 56, 61, 64, 66-67, 74, 80, 82, 92, 96, 98, 101-103, 105, 109, 111, 132, 134, 140, 142, 144, 149, 151, 155, 157, 162, 166, 173, 175, 178, 185
Food, 5, 8, 153, 173, 183-184

Fortune, 156
France, 102, 148, 161-162, 164, 173
Free Will, 74, 76, 152, 162
Freedom, 55, 77, 84, 129, 153, 184
Freemasonry, 30
Friends, 117, 122, 144
Future, 47, 53, 63, 84, 148, 163, 179, 181-182

Gandhi, 140, 142, 163
Genius, 14, 103
Germany, 102, 149, 160, 162-165
Gifts, 27, 132
God, 3, 6, 8-9, 13, 15-16, 18-24, 26-29, 33, 36-37, 39, 41-45, 47-58, 60-66, 70-71, 76-77, 80, 82, 84-85, 89, 91-94, 96, 99, 102-105, 109, 111-118, 121, 126-137, 139, 142-143, 146-147, 149-150, 152-156, 159-160, 162-167, 169-171, 175, 178-179, 182-184, 186
Gold, 4-5, 133, 156, 161-162, 173, 175-176
Golden Age, 167, 172, 179
Government, 26, 146, 149, 151, 163
Great Britain, 148, 161
Greece, 160
Greed, 15, 50, 100, 107, 153-154, 160, 162, 167-168
Groups, 18, 39, 74, 112, 117, 127, 133, 137-138, 140, 143, 170, 185
Gyres, 86

Hall of Learning, 120
Halos, 54
Healer, 16, 90, 142
Healers, 21, 142
Heart, 14, 17, 37, 42, 49, 51, 56, 62, 68, 73, 81, 90, 97, 110, 138-139, 155-156, 159
Hebraic, 20, 35
Hierarchy, 27, 62, 117, 150, 168, 173-174

Hitler, 60, 147, 164
Holy Ghost, 22
Homosexual, 80
Homosexuality, 79
Horoscope, 109
Humanity, 6, 8-9, 12-17, 19-25, 27-30, 33-35, 38-39, 44, 46-48, 51, 55, 57-61, 63, 67, 70-71, 75-79, 81-83, 86, 88-89, 91-92, 99, 102-103, 105-106, 109-114, 116-119, 121, 124-125, 127-133, 137, 139-140, 144, 148-154, 156-157, 159, 164, 167-169, 171-172, 179, 182-186
Humble, 25, 40, 136
Humility, 105, 126, 146, 152-153, 157, 161
Hylos, 4
Hypocrisy, 132

Idolatry, 117
Iliad, 104
Immortality, 27-28, 46, 81
India, 32-33, 39, 149, 160, 163, 165
Indians, 174-176, 178-179
Initiate, 28, 33, 123, 142
Initiates, 102, 115, 140, 142
Inspiration, 49, 61, 98, 101-103, 115, 117, 126, 138-139
Intelligent, 1, 53, 88-89, 126, 151
Interplanetary, 185
Intuition, 53, 58, 66, 75, 92, 111, 116-117, 131
Iron Age, 179
Israelites, 26
Italy, 160, 163

Japanese, 164
Jehovah, 60
Jesus, 7, 11, 13-14, 16-17, 19-40, 62, 72, 92, 97, 102, 111-113, 130, 140, 142

Jew, 17, 20
Jews, 18, 20, 91-92, 177
John, 16, 25, 141
Joseph, 25-26, 179
Judah, 26
Jung, 73
Jupiter, 19

Kabbala, 35
Kindness, 3, 5, 17, 29, 81, 123, 129, 137, 139, 167
Kingdom, 3-9, 14, 19, 26, 29, 41-42, 50, 60-61, 68, 72, 77, 79, 88-89, 116, 126, 136, 139, 156, 162, 174, 181-183
Knowledge, 6-7, 22, 32-34, 44-46, 49-50, 55, 58, 61, 63, 67-68, 70-72, 74-75, 80, 83-85, 87-90, 92-93, 96-98, 100-102, 104, 108, 110, 113, 116-117, 122-123, 126, 135, 141, 147-148, 153-154, 163, 165, 184

Lao-Tse, 140
Law, 1, 8-9, 12-13, 20-21, 51-54, 58, 68, 75, 77, 79-80, 83, 88, 95-96, 104, 118, 126, 130-132, 134, 150, 162-163, 165-166, 173, 185
Laws, 1-2, 4, 8, 20-21, 23, 27, 32, 37, 42-43, 48, 50-53, 59, 63, 67, 70, 72, 75, 77, 83, 86, 89, 115, 118, 120, 122, 126, 130, 137, 142, 144, 147, 151-153, 165, 175
Lesbianism, 79
Light, 11-12, 15, 19, 36, 50, 61, 74, 88, 98, 112-113, 144, 150, 179, 185
Lincoln, 141
Literature, 103-105, 160
Love, 3, 14, 39, 45, 49, 56-57, 62, 76, 80-81, 86, 89-90, 102-103, 118, 122, 127, 130, 137-139, 146, 155, 162, 164, 167, 182, 186
Luther, 142

Magnetism, 43

Man, 2, 4-8, 12-14, 17-18, 21-22, 25, 27-33, 37-39, 41-44, 46, 49, 51-56, 58-59, 61-63, 66-73, 75, 77-89, 91-93, 96-100, 102-106, 111-119, 121-124, 126-127, 129, 131-132, 134-137, 139, 141, 144, 147-150, 152-155, 157, 159, 162, 165-168, 171, 177, 179-184, 186

Mankind, 6-9, 17-19, 21-22, 28-30, 54, 59, 70, 72, 76, 83, 91, 94, 97-98, 106, 112, 116-117, 133, 139-140, 150, 153-154, 156, 167-168, 171, 180, 183, 186

Mark, 102, 135

Marriage, 78-79

Mary, 17, 24-27, 141-143

Masters, 25, 93, 98, 111, 124, 139, 148-149, 158, 171, 174, 182

Mastership, 74-75, 96, 111, 118, 122, 132, 135, 139, 145

Meditation, 43, 48, 50, 54, 93-96, 98, 101, 137, 182

Memory, 21, 47, 113, 177

Michelangelo, 141

Mind, 2, 8, 17, 22, 30, 39, 45, 47, 52-54, 58, 67-68, 73, 80, 85, 88, 92, 101-102, 105, 107-109, 128-129, 139, 143, 149-150, 156, 165, 171-173, 180

Mineral, 1, 3-5, 8, 12, 14, 68-69, 79

Mission, 13, 24, 35, 63, 84, 91-93, 109, 126, 163, 177, 179

Mithraic, 177-178

Muhammadans, 20

Money, 31, 48, 81, 160

Moon, 10, 79, 164, 184, 186

Mormonism, 178

Music, 65, 93, 103-105

Mysticism, 48, 50, 52, 57, 69, 116, 143

Napoleon, 147

Nature, 3, 5-8, 12, 14, 17-18, 24, 31, 33, 37, 39, 49, 52, 59, 64, 68, 76, 83, 88, 99, 106, 134-135, 140, 143, 153, 180-181

Negro, 172, 174, 176-177

New Age, 19-20, 159

New Dispensation, 55, 168

New Order, 160-161, 165-166, 168
New World, 185
Newton, 88
Nobility, 40

Onanism, 79
Orders, 5, 25, 71, 136, 139-140, 143-144, 177
Organizations, 25, 71, 75, 107, 136, 138-141, 143-145
Osiris, 140

Painting, 65, 104
Palestine, 24, 29, 33
Parents, 79-80, 91, 110
Path, 10, 23, 45, 55, 61, 76, 94, 122-123, 132, 137, 150, 162, 173
Pentagram, 35
Peter, 40, 136
Piscean Age, 20, 25
Plant Kingdom, 4-5, 181-182
Plants, 4-5, 53, 98, 168, 180-181
Poets, 102
Poland, 160, 163-164
Pope, 162-163
Portugal, 167
Power, 12-22, 25, 30, 32, 36-37, 39-40, 44, 50, 53-54, 65, 71-72, 78-82, 87, 90, 98, 105-107, 119, 121, 124, 146-147, 150, 154, 160, 162-164, 169-170, 173, 175, 180, 182, 184
Pray, 49, 58, 64-65, 119
Prayer, 50, 58-59
Prevision, 95
Pride, 153, 161, 163
Priest, 24, 112, 161-162, 177
Progress, 14, 17-19, 34, 38, 41, 44, 58, 61, 63, 73, 75-76, 83, 89, 92, 103, 105-106, 124-

127, 130-131, 151, 153, 166, 168, 171, 179-181, 186
Prophet, 141
Punishment, 55, 65

Race Spirit, 60, 173-176, 178
Ray, 59, 93, 97, 112, 127, 138, 142, 169
Rays, 17, 19, 22, 97, 114, 142, 168
Redeemed, 13, 28
Redeemer, 142
Reincarnation, 47, 79, 148
Religion, 18, 20, 24, 26, 35-36, 40-42, 46, 69, 153-154, 161, 163, 177-178, 182-183
Religions, 23, 30, 41, 62, 143, 177, 182
Renunciation, 54
Reptile Kingdom, 14
Responsibility, 65, 74, 78, 110
Roman, 17, 29, 71, 149, 164
Romans, 31, 60
Rome, 23, 40, 162
Russia, 148-149, 160, 162, 172, 175, 183

Salt, 72
Salvation, 59-60, 78, 144, 161, 169, 172
Saturn, 19
Saved, 13, 92, 167
Savior, 14, 16-17, 22, 140
Scotland, 148
Seasons, 183
Seer, 141
Self, 17, 27, 41, 43-46, 50-51, 54, 61-62, 67, 70, 74, 81-82, 88, 92, 96, 104, 121-122, 128, 130-132, 135-137, 139-140, 143, 154, 171, 181-182
Semitic Race, 20

Sermon on the Mount, 42, 45, 50, 52, 72-73, 89, 113, 135
Serpent, 6, 14-17, 173
Service, 5, 17, 23-24, 61, 107, 111, 126, 129-132, 134, 144, 174, 176
Sex, 12, 14-15, 17, 78, 80-81, 154
Silent Watchers, 119
Sin, 28, 51, 78, 106, 160
Societies, 140, 143
Solar, 3, 12, 14, 16, 19, 81, 138, 175, 177
Son, 13, 18-21, 36, 142, 159, 164, 166-167
Soul, 4, 7, 9-10, 17, 19, 22-23, 41-44, 46-47, 53, 55, 57-60, 64, 70-71, 73-74, 76, 79-80, 83, 88, 90-93, 95-97, 99, 101-102, 104-105, 112-113, 115-117, 120-122, 124-126, 129, 131, 137-138, 143-146, 152-154, 170, 179
Spain, 160-161, 173-174
Spanish, 147, 175
Spiral, 46, 75-76, 94, 98, 147, 186
Spirals, 147
Spirits, 29, 60, 173-175
Spirituality, 19-20, 23, 62, 70, 95, 118, 127, 133, 149, 163
St. John, 141
St. Martin, 141-142
Sweden, 160-161
Swedenborg, 141
Symbology, 17, 95, 132
Symbols, 35, 122-123, 133

Teacher, 12, 16, 32-33, 48, 98, 109-112, 114, 117, 139, 142
Teachers, 33-34, 49, 108, 110-113, 116-117, 121, 142, 179
Theologians, 20
Theology, 53
Therapeuti, 24
Thoughts, 54, 59-60, 64, 82, 93, 95, 99, 106-107, 122, 137-138, 140, 153, 181, 183

Time, 2, 15-18, 21-24, 26-32, 35, 44, 46-53, 64, 72-73, 76, 80-83, 86, 90, 92, 94-95, 98-100, 106, 109, 114, 116, 118-119, 123-124, 130-131, 133, 139, 141-142, 148, 158, 161-164, 166, 169-170, 172, 174, 177, 179-181, 183, 185-186

Transfiguration, 23, 28

Truth, 2, 7, 20-21, 29-30, 38, 41, 46-47, 49-51, 53, 55-56, 62, 64, 68, 76-78, 81, 96-100, 102, 104, 106, 111, 113, 115, 136-138, 149-150, 156, 158, 162, 164, 166, 182

Turkey, 163-164, 172

Turks, 119

Twelve, 26, 32, 37-38, 138-139, 149

United States, 160, 162-163, 165

Universal, 62, 75, 131, 137, 144, 154-155, 158, 161

Universe, 1-2, 4, 9-10, 19, 28, 51-53, 61, 64, 68, 70, 83, 86, 89, 96, 101, 103, 118, 130-131, 134, 137, 153-154, 163, 165-166, 180, 182, 184

Unmoved Mover, 68

Vatican, 33, 162-163

Virgin, 17, 21, 24-25

Vivisection, 65

Wagner, 88

Wales, 148

War, 147, 152, 159-162, 165, 167, 170, 172, 176, 183

Water, 4, 25, 71-72, 97, 165

Weakness, 107, 152

Weaknesses, 152

Weather, 106, 170

White Race, 178-179

Whitman, 141

Whoring, 79

Will, 2, 6-8, 12-13, 18-23, 28, 30-31, 33, 38, 40-45, 47-65, 67-69, 71-74, 76-83, 88-107, 109-119, 121-143, 146-157, 159-172, 174-186

Wine, 55, 81
Wisdom, 12-13, 15, 19, 22, 60, 76, 84, 87, 89, 92, 94-95, 103, 114, 128, 138-139, 157, 160-161, 168, 180
Women, 24, 32, 101, 139, 158, 179
Work, 18, 23, 30-31, 33, 37-39, 47, 55, 58-59, 75-78, 80, 82-84, 90, 92-93, 95, 100-102, 104, 110-111, 116-117, 121, 124-127, 129-132, 134-137, 139-141, 144-145, 149, 155, 165, 168-170, 174, 179, 185
Writers, 102, 141
Yeshua, 26
Zarathustra, 113, 140